D1316743

EveryDay American

EveryDay American

WHAT YOU CAN DO FOR YOUR COUNTRY—TODAY AND EVERY DAY

Cheri Sicard

MADISON
PARK
PRESS™

NEW YORK

Published by Madison Park Press, One Penn Plaza, New York, NY 10119. Madison Park Press is a trademark of Bertelsmann Direct North America, Inc.

Book design by Tiffany Kukec

ISBN: 978-1-58288-297-0

Printed in the United States of America

To my late parents, Lester and Bessie Sicard, and my older sisters, Bambi Burnes and Linda McWilliams, who not only instilled in me a love of our country at a young age, they took me by the hand and showed me why it was so great.

ACKNOWLEDGMENTS

My sincere thanks to the following people who helped with the process of writing this book, or put up with me while I did it: Chuck Burnes, Mitch Mandell, Gary Stewart, Richard and Tracy Burnes, Janet Rosen, and Sheree Bykofsky.

CONTENTS

Introduction xiii

GET INVOLVED

Buy American 3

Be an Informed Consumer 4

Pay Your Taxes 10

Serve on a Jury 12

Support the American Red Cross 14

Spend Money/Invest Wisely in a Healthy Economy 16

Fill Out Your Census Forms 18

Buy Savings Bonds and Invest in America 21

Consider a Career in the Military 24

Serve in the Reserves 29

Register with Selective Services 31

Support Our Men and Women in Uniform 34

Remember Our POWs and MIAs 36

Be an Informed Voter 39

Contact Your Elected Officials 42

Register for a Political Party 44

Use the Internet to Get Politically Active 46

Apply for a Presidential Appointment 49

Campaign 52

Reduce America's Oil Dependence 54

Recycle, Reuse, Conserve 58

Safeguard America's Agriculture 60

Safeguard America's Water Supply and
   Our Environment 61

Think Globally, Act Locally 64

Be Smokey Bear's Friend and
   Help Prevent Forest Fires 67

Be Prepared for Emergencies
   and National Disasters 69

Help Eliminate Hunger 73

Join AmeriCorps 74

Join the Peace Corps 78

Help the FBI Fight Crime 81

Use the Freedom of Information Act (FOIA)
   and the Privacy Act 84

Help Airport Security 89

Become a Permanent Resident
   or Naturalized Citizen 92

Volunteer 95

BE INFORMED

Learn About the Constitution 101

Learn About the Constitutional Amendments 105

Learn How Laws Are Enacted 110

Learn the Chain of Command of the United States ... 113

Understand How the United States Government
    Is Structured 115

Understand How and Why the Electoral College
    System Elects Our President 119

Understand Campaign Finance 122

Learn About the CIA 126

Learn About NASA 128

Use the Library of Congress 132

Learn About Social Security 134

Know Your Presidents 140

Know the United States Territories and Possessions 141

Learn About Our National Motto 146

Know the American's Creed 147

Learn About Our National Symbol 149

Learn About the Great Seal of the United States 152

Get News from a Variety of Sources 155

Be an Informed Traveler 157

Three Essential Web Resources for Americans 159

CELEBRATE

Presidents Day 163

George Washington's Birthday 168

Abraham Lincoln's Birthday 172

Martin Luther King Jr.'s Birthday 175

Memorial Day 178

Have a Safe and Happy Independence Day 181

Honor Veterans on Veterans Day 183

Arbor Day 188

Visit Our Nation's Capital 190

Visit the Statue of Liberty and Ellis Island 195

Visit Our National Parks 200

Take In the Treasures of the Smithsonian Institution . . . 204

Sing the National Anthem 208

Top Ten Patriotic Music Selections 211

Display the National Flower 214

Bake an Apple Pie 215

APPENDIX A

Flag Etiquette 221

APPENDIX B

The Declaration of Independence 235

The Constitution 241

INTRODUCTION

WHAT MAKES A GOOD American? It depends on who you ask. The paths to patriotism are legion and what's right for one person may not be appropriate for another. But that's all right—this is America, where we have the fundamental right to be different. And different we are, but sometimes we're more alike than we care to admit. For instance, all our political parties share more or less the same general vision and beliefs—in their hearts, their members all want a stronger, safer, better America for this generation and those to come. Most all of them believe in the United States Constitution. The differences come from how people interpret their beliefs and how they work to bring about their visions.

Much of my childhood was spent on extended road trips that criss-crossed the United States. Part of my family were circus performers (no, I'm not kidding), and the other part just loved to travel and go along for the ride. By the time I was 12, I was lucky enough to have visited nearly every state in the union. From a child's eye view, the areas of the United States might well have been different nations—they had different geographical terrains, different climates, different foods, different industries, not to mention populations of ethnically diverse people who not only looked different, but talked differently and had distinctly different needs, opinions, and lifestyles. But one thing united all the people I saw—they were all Americans. When the national anthem was played before the start of a performance, many in the crowd would sing along; others silently and solemnly observed, hands over hearts; and if you looked closely, you could always spot a sentimental tear or two.

Where else in the world could you find such an amalgam of varying races, religions, ethnic backgrounds, and social classes? Yet with all their differences, Americans know that they can and will unite to support, protect, and honor the single nation they all love. Sometimes patriotism shows itself in times of tragedy and loss, like after the events of September 11, 2001, and sometimes it shows itself in something as simple and innocent as a group of strangers gathered together at a ball game, circus, or Fourth of July celebration to sing the national anthem.

So what makes a good American? It depends who you ask. In the end, I think it's not important what your political views are—what's important is that you have some. Thomas Jefferson believed that it takes an involved citizenry to make democracy work. While they may not realize it, citizens of the United States have the fundamental right to alter or even abolish their government or amend their Constitution. This may all sound rather revolutionary, and with good reason—our Founding Fathers came up with the idea after fighting for independence from the British.

You exercise your fundamental constitutional right by casting an informed vote on election day. Votes created our government, and they can also change it. So, at the very basic level, a good American is an informed voter. Of course, there's so much more you can do to go beyond that, but patriotism begins in the voting booth.

Throughout this book you'll find lots of information about U.S. history and government that all Americans should know, but often don't. You'll also find enough trivia, tidbits, and Americana to dazzle your friends as a seemingly unending font of patriotic knowledge. More importantly, you'll discover lots of ways you can actively work to make America a better place, support our men and women in uniform, and take an active part in our governmental process. Not all suggestions are appropriate, or even possible, for all people. But that's all right, too. This is America. You can decide which ways you can best serve and celebrate your country.

To help you locate the kind of information you need quickly, you'll find chapters in this book arranged into three main categories:

- **Get Involved**   These are action items that ordinary citizens can do to help the United States.

- **Be Informed**   Too many Americans lack fundamental knowledge about their history, and the way the government works. These short entries will give you a quick overview of important information every American should know.

- **Celebrate**   As Americans we have lots of reasons to celebrate and honor our country. These entries will teach you about the history and traditions behind America's patriotic celebrations and offer ideas on how to get the most out of living in the U.S.A.

So browse, read, enjoy, and most of all, get informed, get involved, and celebrate. This is your country, do something for it!

GET INVOLVED

Buy American

IF YOU PROFESS TO support your country, there's no better way to put your money where your mouth is than to buy products made in America. Consumer dollars provide the most direct way to invest in America's economy. Not only do American companies create jobs for Americans, they pay substantially more taxes than their foreign counterparts.

A subcategory of buying American-made products is "look for the union label," which assures the consumer of not only quality merchandise, but promotes justice on the job. The union label on products signifies that labor and management have signed a binding contract, making a "win–win/win–win" arrangement for labor, management, consumers, and America. The theory is that the economy benefits not only from goods sold, but also from the paychecks and taxes of well-paid workers.

ADDITIONAL INFORMATION

- Made in the USA—An online database of American-made products at *www.madeinusa.org*.

- Shop American—Over 40,000 products from over 700 vendors, all made in America, including merchandise that benefits American charities such as the American Red Cross and the Salvation Army, at *www.buyamerican.com*.

- AFL-CIO listing of union-made products and services at *www.ShopUnionMade.org.*

- *How to Buy American* by Roger Simmermaker. While it may seem like a simple task to buy American, it often isn't, as many companies who appear to be American are actually subsidiaries of foreign businesses. This handy guidebook will help you know the difference. Look for it at your favorite bookstore or online at *www.howtobuyamerican.com,* or phone 1-888-US-OWNED to order.

Be an Informed Consumer

IF YOU FEEL FISCALLY challenged, the U.S. government wants to help you learn to manage your money better and be an informed, socially conscious consumer. The Federal Consumer Information Center (FCIC) in Pueblo, Colorado, serves as a trusted, one-stop source for answers to consumer questions about federal agencies, programs, and services by helping other federal agencies develop, promote, and distribute useful information to the public. Their trained staff can answer consumer questions in English or Spanish, and if they don't have the answer, they'll try to direct you to someone who does.

Established in 1970 as a separately funded operation within the U.S. General Services Administration, the Federal Consumer Information Center maintains close ties with more than 100 different federal offices, agencies, and departments, as well as many consumer and trade organizations. The center's *Consumer Information Catalog* lists titles, descriptions, and ordering information for the more than 200 free and low-cost publications. Before you make any major (or even somewhat major) purchase, it's smart to check out the free consumer information Uncle Sam has prepared to help you. You can get advice on how to make smart shopping decisions on everything from used cars to children's toys, learn how to buy insurance, protect your investments, establish a productive relationship with your bank, and much, much more. The millions of Americans who request FCIC publications each year can't be wrong.

While the staff of the FCIC doesn't handle consumer complaints themselves, their *Consumer Action Handbook* can guide you through the process of writing an effective complaint letter and educate you with pre-purchase information and other advice to help prevent and solve consumer marketplace problems. You'll always know just who to contact too, as the *Handbook* includes contact information for thousands of corporations, trade groups, state and local consumer protection offices, and federal agencies.

- To download free copies of the *Consumer Information Catalog* or the *Consumer Action Handbook* visit *www.pueblo.gsa.gov*. You can also order the publication by phone by calling toll-free 1-888-8-PUEBLO.

- For general information, the public can access the FCIC information call center by calling 1-800-688-9889 (TTY 1-800-326-2996) between 9 a.m. and 8 p.m. *EDT*.

HELP FIGHT ONLINE FRAUD

The *Consumer Sentinel*, maintained by the Federal Trade Commission (FTC), serves as a one-stop complaint database where consumers can log complaints about companies they believe have done them wrong, cases of identity theft, overseas consumer transactions gone wrong, and even "spam" e-mail. While the FTC does not resolve individual consumer problems, they do compile the complaints into a secure online database used worldwide by hundreds of civil and criminal law enforcement agencies, who access the information through an encrypted web site. Your valuable input helps fraud investigations from Internet scams to telemarketing cons. Online since 1997, the *Consumer Sentinel* now houses over a million consumer fraud complaints. To log a consumer complaint visit *www.consumer.gov/sentinel*.

SOCIALLY CONSCIOUS SHOPPING

Why not use your consumer power to help a worthy cause while purchasing the products and services you need? The Internet is making it easier than ever to make your consumer dollars really count. By accessing your favorite Internet shopping sites through the portals below, all you have to do is shop, click, search, or sign up for services like you always do, but this time a portion of your purchases will help generate millions of dollars in donations for charities. What an easy, convenient, and painless way to support your favorite charities!

- *www.igive.com* By shopping through iGive.com, you can make purchases at over 680 favorite online retailers like Amazon.com, Sharper Image, Target, and Martha Stewart, while up to 26 percent of each purchase gets donated to your favorite worthy cause. As of this writing, over $2,623,987.07 has been raised for over 37,412 charities from high school marching bands to local animal shelters, community food banks, and breast cancer research. You can even add your own favorite charity to the iGive.com list of qualified causes.

- *www.schoolpop.com* SchoolPop works much like iGive.com, with the emphasis on helping schools by bringing more than 300 store, catalog, and online merchants together with parents and the community to raise money for K-12 schools nationwide. To date, SchoolPop.com has raised over $200 million for over 30,000 schools and other nonprofits nationwide.

- *www.greatergood.com* Up to 15 percent of every purchase made through GreaterGood.com goes to the Greater Good charity of your choice. Your consumer dollars can support the Elizabeth Glaser Pediatric AIDS Foundation, Big Brothers and Big Sisters, the Nature Conservancy, the Muscular Dystrophy Association, or over 3,000 other worthy charities.

ADDITIONAL INFORMATION

Government Consumer Information—The Government's Internet hub with links to all kinds of important consumer information at *www.consumer.gov*.

☆ *The Scope of Information*

Pssst! Don't overlook this chapter. The scope and quality of the free government publications available through the Federal Consumer Information Center in Pueblo, Colorado, truly boggles the mind. Before you spend money on books, check the center's Web site first. Uncle Sam may have already prepared the information you're looking for. You can read the reports free over the Internet or order print copies (sometimes a minimal fee is involved, sometimes the publications are free). Here's just a tiny sampling of the topics covered in FCIC publications.

- **Fishing Is Fun for Everyone**   What equipment you'll need, what kind of bait to use, how to cast and tie knots, and where to fish for more information.

- **Swindlers Are Calling**   Eight things you should know about telemarketing fraud, nine tip-offs that a caller could be a crook, and ten ways to avoid becoming a victim.

- **Taking Legal Action**   When legal action may be appropriate, how to file in small claims court, and when to consider hiring a lawyer.

- **Finding the Best Used Car**   What to look for on the test drive, warning signs of hidden damage, and how to verify the vehicle's history.

- **Nine Ways to Lower Your Auto Insurance Costs**   Tips on what to do to lower your expenses, including a chart to compare discounts.

- **Helping Your Overweight Child**   The path to good nutrition and health for parents of an overweight child, or those who are concerned about their child's eating habits.

- **Parents' Guide to the Internet**   Information on equipment and software, costs, surfing the Internet, getting e-mail, and protecting your privacy, including interesting and fun online resources for parents and children.

- **Internet Auctions: A Guide for Buyers and Sellers** How Internet auctions work, payment options, and how to protect yourself.

- **Buying a Computer** Practical advice on how to buy a computer that fits your needs, with tips on protecting your computer and data.

- **Nontraditional Education: Alternative Ways to Earn Your Credentials** How to get high school or college credit through the GED program, the National External Diploma program, correspondence and distance study, and standardized tests.

- **Changing Your Job** How to find out if your current job is right for you, what to do when you look for a new job, and what happens to your benefits when you change jobs.

- **Cooking for Groups: A Volunteer's Guide to Food Safety** Learn how to cook and serve food safely and avoid foodborne illness for any type of group, whether it's a family reunion buffet or community cookout.

- **Recipes and Tips for Healthy, Thrifty Meals** Tips on planning meals and making shopping lists, complete with a sample two-week menu and 40 great recipes.

- **Snack Smart for Healthy Teeth** Tips on choosing the right snacks to prevent tooth decay and promote healthy eating, with a list of suggested items from the five basic food groups.

- **How to Hold Your Own Against Colds and Flu** The facts on lowering your chance of infection, treating difficult cold and flu symptoms, and knowing when to see a doctor.

- **How to Buy a Home with a Low Down Payment** How to qualify for a low down payment mortgage and determine what you can afford, with an explanation of how mortgage insurance works.

- **Copyright Basics** What can be copyrighted, who can apply, registration procedures, filing fees, what forms to use, and more.

- **Your Trip Abroad** Information and a helpful checklist of necessary documents and things to arrange before, during, and after your trip overseas.

Pay Your Taxes

As much as everyone hates to do it, paying your taxes is an important part of being a good American. The money the federal government needs to pay its bills comes largely from taxes. For instance, in fiscal year 2001:

- Individual income taxes raised an estimated $972 billion, equal to about 9.7 percent of the gross domestic product (GDP).

- Social insurance payroll taxes include Social Security taxes, Medicare taxes, unemployment insurance taxes, and federal employee retirement payments. This category has grown from 2 percent of GDP in 1955 to an estimated 6.8 percent in 2001.

- Corporate income taxes, which raised an estimated $195 billion, have shrunk steadily as a percentage of GDP, from 4.5 percent in 1955 to an estimated 1.9 percent in 2001.

- Excise taxes apply to various products, including alcohol, tobacco, transportation fuels, and telephone services. The government earmarks some of these taxes to support certain activities—including highways and airports—and deposits others in the general fund.

- The government also collects estate and gift taxes, customs duties, and miscellaneous revenues such as Federal Reserve earnings, fines, penalties, and forfeitures.

TAXING TIMES

The Internal Revenue Service, a branch of the Department of Treasury, serves as our country's tax collection agency. Its beginnings go back to 1862 and the Civil War, when Congress, under President Abraham Lincoln, created the Commissioner of Internal Revenue and imposed an income tax to help pay war expenses.

The tax was repealed 10 years later. But Congress liked the idea, so they revived the income tax in 1894. The Supreme Court ruled income tax unconstitutional the following year, but in 1913, the 16th Amendment gave Congress the authority to enact an income tax again.

Today the IRS directly deals with more Americans than any other institution, public or private. In 2006, the agency collected $1,236,259,371,000 in individual income taxes and assisted more than 63 million taxpayers who called the toll-free automated telephone line, wrote letters, or visited one of the more than 400 IRS offices nationwide. As much as citizens like to complain about the agency, it does hold the honor of being one of the world's most efficient tax agencies. In 2000, the agency collected more than $2 trillion in revenue and processed 226 million tax returns, costing taxpayers only 39 cents for each $100 collected.

The IRS's mission statement says it seeks to provide America's taxpayers with top quality service by helping them understand and meet their tax responsibilities and by applying the tax law with integrity and fairness to all. In that spirit, customer service representatives can be reached toll-free at 1-800-829-1040, Monday through Friday from 7 a.m. to 10 p.m. You can also get lots of tax information as well as IRS forms and publications online at *www.irs.gov*.

ADDITIONAL INFORMATION

Learn how your taxes are spent by studying the federal budget at *www.whitehouse.gov/omb/budget*.

Serve on a Jury

JURORS PERFORM AN ESSENTIAL role in sustaining the American system of justice, and jury duty is an important responsibility of every

U.S. citizen. The right to a trial by a jury of one's peers is guaranteed in our Constitution, and a jury's honest and impartial decision helps protect our fundamental rights to fair and efficient justice for all.

While 6 or 12 citizens normally compose the typical jury, courts usually summon between 35 to 75 potential jurors for each trial, knowing that not all jurors will be suitable for all cases. Participation in jury duty usually lasts for a week. Being called for jury duty does not guarantee you will be selected to actually serve during that time—you must simply be available to serve on a jury, if needed. Of course, if you're assigned to a long ongoing public trial (think of the O. J. Simpson or Phil Spector cases) you may be required to serve for much longer.

You can't volunteer for jury service, but as long as you are a registered voter you can reasonably expect to be called to serve every year or two. (You won't be asked to serve more than once per year.) Failure to report for jury duty after you receive a summons can bring serious consequences and expensive fines, so never ignore one. In certain instances, you may be excused from jury duty because of scheduling or employment conflicts, illness, or other hardships, but be prepared to have a darn good excuse. The courts take citizens' jury responsibilities very seriously, but will usually try to accommodate postponement requests.

JURY ELIGIBILITY REQUIREMENTS

Certain requirements vary slightly from district to district, but these rules usually hold true:

- Jurors must be U.S. citizens, either born or naturalized.

- Jurors must be at least 18 years old and reside in the county of their jury service.

- Jurors must be able to read and write.

- Jurors must be of sound mind.

In addition, potential jurors usually cannot be convicted felons (unless their rights have been restored) or be on probation, deferred adjudication, or under indictment for a felony.

Support the American Red Cross

THE AMERICAN RED CROSS, part of the International Red Cross and Red Crescent movement, works to save lives and ease suffering, both locally and globally. In addition to offering health and safety training, the American Red Cross supplies relief services to communities across the country in the aftermath of earthquakes, tornadoes, floods, fires, hurricanes, and other disasters. They are also responsible for half the nation's blood supply and blood products.

The American Red Cross operates independently of the U.S. government, although it works closely with government agencies during times of major crises. In 1905, Congress granted a charter to the American Red Cross that required it to act "in accord with the military authorities as a medium of communication between the people of the United States and their armed forces." Ever since, the American Red Cross has been providing humanitarian services to members of the U.S. military and their families around the world. Living and working in the same difficult and dangerous environment as our troops, the Red Cross gives comfort to soldiers and provides emergency message services (about deaths and births, for example), comfort kits, and blank cards for the troops to send home to loved ones.

Red Cross organizations do not discriminate on the basis of nationality, race, religious beliefs, class, or political opinions. There can be only one Red Cross or Red Crescent Society in any country, and it must be open to all and carry on its humanitarian work throughout the entire country. National societies, like the American Red Cross, while subject to the laws of their countries, must always maintain their autonomy in order to uphold the principles of the International Red Cross movement.

Although the red cross is not a religious symbol, some societies view it that way; therefore, the symbol of the red crescent is used instead of the cross in most Islamic countries. The Red Shield of David represents the organization in Israel.

HELP THE RED CROSS

Although chartered by Congress, the Red Cross does not receive any government financial assistance. Individuals wishing to make a financial donation to the American Red Cross may send a check to their local Red Cross chapter or to:

American Red Cross
P.O. Box 37243
Washington, DC 20013

Donors may also call 1-800-RED-CROSS (1-800-733-2767), or 1-800-257-7575 for help in Spanish, to charge a financial contribution to their credit cards. Donations may also be made online at the American Red Cross secure Web site, *www.redcross.org*.

People who want to volunteer their time and talents should contact their local American Red Cross chapter, as the vast majority of volunteer opportunities are typically found within the local community. International disaster relief workers are drawn from a pool of paid and volunteer staff with extensive prior experience.

If you wish to help by donating blood, call your local Red Cross Blood Services office or 1-800-GIVE-LIFE for more information.

Spend Money/Invest Wisely in a Healthy Economy

AMERICANS ARE CONSTANTLY HEARING about how it's their patriotic duty to spend money to keep the economy moving. In some cases that's good advice, as consumer spending is an important barometer of an economy's strength. But let's examine the idea a little deeper. Spending money to help boost the American economy is a good idea for both you and the country if, and only if, you can afford it. If you don't have to buy on credit and you have enough put away for emergencies, then spend away. On the other hand, you're not helping anyone if you use patriotism as an excuse to go on a buying binge that will leave you burdened with credit card debt. By borrowing money you'll have to struggle to repay, you can actually become a burden to the very society you want to help.

The flip side of spending money to boost the economy, for those who aren't in a position to do so, is to work toward eliminating personal debt. Imagine how much you could spend each month if you didn't have any credit card bills! The first step to creating a healthy economy is to get a hold on your own personal finances.

WHAT IS A DOLLAR WORTH?

Because of inflation, the value of money changes over time. Ten dollars in 1952 would buy you considerably more goods and services than 10 dollars in 2008. If it seems like your paycheck isn't going as far as it used to, it's not your imagination. The Consumer Price Index (CPI) is a measure of the average change in prices over time in a market, and a fun web tool at *minneapolisfed.org/research/data/us/calc* lets you instantly compare the value of money across time. Just type in the year and dollar amounts you want to compare. For instance, goods and services that cost $1.00 back in 1913 would set you back a whopping $20.84 in 2007!

ADDITIONAL INFORMATION

- Government Consumer Information—Government Internet hub with links to all kinds of important consumer information at *www.consumer.gov*.

- Economy at a Glance—The Bureau of Labor Statistics Web site lets you look up the economic status of the country by region, state, or metropolitan area, including labor force data and consumer price indexes, at *www.bls.gov/eag*.

- Employment and Unemployment Statistics Nationwide—More from the Bureau of Labor Statistics at *www.bls.gov/lau*.

GET OUT OF DEBT

The following Web sites have great consumer information and tips for getting and staying out of debt:

- The Motley Fool—*www.fool.com/credit/credit.htm*

- About.com Credit/Debt Management Resources—
  www.credit.about.com

FRUGAL LIVING

Get out of debt faster with these Web sites offering tips and ideas for making your money stretch as far as it can go:

- The Dollar Stretcher—*www.stretcher.com/index.cfm*

- About.com Frugal Living Web Resources—*www.frugalliving.about.com*

- Frugal Mom—*www.frugalmom.net*

Fill Out Your Census Forms

EVERY TEN YEARS THE U.S. government goes on a fact-finding mission of enormous proportions, sending out census forms to the more than 105 million households in the United States. Uncle Sam wants to know how many people live in each house as well as their ages, sex, and race.

No, the government isn't nosy—the sole purpose of census surveys is to secure general statistical information. The replies you provide on your census form enable the compilation of general statistics.

The government takes the confidentiality of census replies seriously. By law, no census taker or any other Census Bureau employee is permitted to reveal identifiable information about any person, household, or business. The law also prohibits schedules and questionnaires from any census from being released for 72 years. Even then, only the heirs or legal representatives of the named individuals can gain access.

The broad census profile of the people who make up this nation helps the government determine how best to serve the nation. For instance, a town with a growing population of people under the age of 18 will likely need more schools, but a town with a growing population of senior citizens would benefit from better public transportation services.

Beyond government services, the census impacts American citizens in an even greater way—it plays an important role in upholding democracy. Every state sends two people to the Senate, but the House of Representatives differs: The number of representatives a state sends to the House is based on the state's population. For an accurate count of the state's population, the government turns to—you guessed it—the census.

It's easy to see why filling out census forms is such an important responsibility for citizens—if you neglect to complete your census forms, you may be helping to cheat your local community of the representation it deserves and the public services it needs.

★ *History of the Census*

Following America's independence from England, there was an almost immediate need for a census of our new nation, and Article I of our Constitution requires a census be taken every 10 years. The first census, conducted in 1790, counted the population at 3.9 million. By comparison, the 2001 census counts that number at a whopping 281,421,906.

As the country grew, our needs became more complex. The statistical help provided by the census guided the government's planning for America's needs. Over the years, the census questions evolved with the country's growth and progress. In 1810, the first inquiries on manufactures and quantity and value of products were added; in 1840, the census added questions about fisheries; and the 1850 census included questions on social issues like taxation, churches, pauperism, and crime. In fact, there were so many questions in the censuses of 1880 and 1890 that it took the government almost a full decade to publish all the results. In the case of the 1890 census, much of the work is now lost—a devastating fire in 1921 destroyed 99 percent of the records.

The Census Bureau of the Digital Age offers American citizens far greater efficiency. The results of the 2000 census are currently available. The Census Bureau's Web site at *www.census.gov* offers an encyclopedia of statistical knowledge about the United States, plus it's a fun place to surf to simply check out "fast facts" about your state or region or the United States in general.

SAVINGS BONDS ARE ESSENTIALLY a loan that bond purchasers make to the United States. As the full faith and credit of the U.S. government backs these bonds, they are one of the safest investments an individual can make. Interest earned on U.S. savings bonds is exempt from state and local income tax, and you can also defer paying federal income tax on the interest until you cash in your bond or until it stops earning interest in 30 years. If lost, stolen, or destroyed, bonds can be replaced.

WHO CAN PURCHASE BONDS?

- Residents of the United States, its territories, and possessions.

- Citizens of the United States who live abroad.

- Civilian employees of the United States and members of the armed services (regardless of residence or citizenship, provided they have a valid Social Security number).

- Residents of Canada and Mexico who work in the United States, but only through payroll savings plans set up by their employers.

THE TWO TYPES OF SAVINGS BONDS

Series EE bonds are sold for terms totaling 30 years. Their value increases as a fixed-rate interest is added to the principal. Both principal and interest are paid in a single lump sum when the bond is redeemed. You can purchase Series EE bonds through any local financial institution serving as a savings bond agent or online from the government's Treasury Direct Web site. At the former, agents accept applications and payment for bonds, then forward them to a Federal Reserve bank where the bonds are issued and mailed to the purchaser within 15 business days. So that no interest is lost, the bond's issue date reflects the date of application.

Series I bonds are an accrual-type security that earn interest from the date of purchase. After buying the bond for the face amount ($50 to $10,000), Series I bonds increase in value monthly. The interest is paid when you redeem the bond. Interest earnings rates are a combination of a fixed rate and an inflation adjusted rate.

In both cases individuals are limited to buying no more than $30,000 in bonds per calendar year. You can redeem bonds at any time after a 12-month minimum holding period, although if you redeem them before they're five years old, you'll forfeit the three most recent months' interest; at or after five years there is no penalty for cashing out your bonds.

PATRIOT BONDS

In response to public desire to support the current war against terrorism, Series EE bonds bought on or after December 11, 2001, will be inscribed with the special legend "Patriot Bond." The change is strictly cosmetic: There is no difference between the Patriot Bond and a regular Series EE bond. The funds are not earmarked for the war effort, but still go into the general fund.

SAVINGS BONDS AS GIFTS

Bonds make great gifts for any occasion—birthdays, weddings, graduations, births, special holidays—the list is endless. Since bonds are available in denominations from $50 to $10,000, there's a bond for almost every budget. Even if you don't have the Social Security number of the recipient, you can still buy the bond using your own number without incurring tax liability—the numbers are used solely for tracking purposes, should the bond be lost or stolen. Bonds bought as gifts do not count toward your annual buying limit of $30,000. Plan ahead three weeks if you want the bond to be delivered to you. If you don't have that much time, buy directly online for quicker service. Your gift bond can even be "delivered" to the recipient electronically. The Treasury department also offers a gift certificate you can print using your computer until the authentic documents arrive.

ADDITIONAL INFORMATION

- The official government savings bond site with everything you could want to know about savings bonds, including current rates, online purchasing, and more is at *www.savingsbond.gov*.

- Savings Bonds for Kids is a fun site designed to teach children all about bonds and investing in America: *www.savingsbond.gov/sav/savkids.htm*.

- Find a detailed comparison of Series EE and Series I bonds at *www.savingsbond.gov/indiv/research/indepth/ebonds/res_e_bonds_e ecomparison.htm*.

- Buy gift bonds online at *www.treasurydirect.gov/indiv/planning/plan_gifts.htm*.

- U.S. savings bonds may provide tax savings when used to finance higher education; for more information visit *www.treasurydirect.gov/indiv/planning/plan_education.htm*.

Consider a Career in the Military

WITH OVER 750,000 PEOPLE in the armed forces, the U.S. military is one of the world's largest employers—and with little wonder. A career in the military offers many rewards and benefits, not the least of which is the satisfaction of knowing you are honorably serving your country. In addition to active duty and reserve personnel, the military employs civilians in thousands of jobs, so you don't even have to enlist to work for the defense of our country.

BENEFITS OF A MILITARY CAREER

- **Job Training**   Regardless of rank, everyone in the military is trained in a job specialty. Since military jobs usually have civilian counterparts, you'll leave the service with marketable skills.

- **Education While in the Military**   The military encourages you to advance your higher education by paying up to 100 percent of the tab for approved courses at accredited colleges, universities, and commercial schools. Additionally, some military schools allow you to earn college credits as you learn on the job.

- **Education After Service**   The education benefits offered by the military are too enticing for many recruits to resist. The Montgomery GI Bill gives $37,224 for college or vocational training to anyone who completes a 36-month enlistment. Furthermore, if you also qualify for the Marine Corps or Coast Guard College Funds, or the Army or Navy College Fund Program, a recruit can virtually pay for his or her entire education.

- **Student Loan Help**   If you're a college graduate with student loans to repay, the Army will repay $1,500 or 33 percent of an eligible student loan—whichever is greater—up to a maximum of $70,000 for each year you agree to serve during your first tour of duty. The Navy's financial assistance programs pay up to $65,000 per year while a recruit is completing his or her undergraduate studies, provided that they meet certain academic requirements. As both these programs come with substantial restrictions, check with your recruiter for further details.

- **Free Health Care**   Active duty military members receive complete medical and dental care at no cost. Military personnel's families may also enroll in military health care, although small enrollment fees and annual deductible fees may apply.

- **Salary and Tax Benefits**   Military personnel are paid twice a month. In addition to base pay, an armed forces member may be eligible for certain types of additional allowances such as housing, uniforms, cost of living adjustments, or overseas pay. Military base pay is subject to regular federal and state income taxes, but all additional earnings and allowances are not taxed.

- **Paid Vacations**   Military personnel receive 30 days full paid vacation per year.

- **Regular Promotions**   The military recognizes hard work and promotes people based on their knowledge and experience in their chosen fields, their performance, their time served, and the needs of the service.

- **Life Insurance**   Active duty military may elect to protect their families and buy up to $400,000 in Service Group Life Insurance at substantially reduced rates.

- **Discount Shopping**   Active duty military members may shop at base stores for groceries and general department store goods at significantly reduced prices.

- **Retirement**   Non-disabled military personnel have three retirement choices, and the date when you first join, along with personal financial considerations, will help determine your options. In addition to financial compensation, retired military personnel who have completed at least 15 years of active duty service may still take advantage of base facilities such as medical care and reduced rate shopping. To help figure out what retirement plan would be best for you, visit *www.defenselink.mil/militarypay/retirement/index.html*.

WHERE DO I SIGN UP?

Join the Army   Applicants must be 17 to 42 years old, U.S. citizens or registered aliens, healthy, and in good physical condition. All applicants must take the Armed Services Vocational Aptitude Battery (ASVAB), offered at most high schools, to determine which careers they are best suited for. To become a commissioned army officer, a candidate must attend the U.S. Military Academy or the army's Officer Candidate School, have participated in the Army Reserve Officers' Training Corps (ROTC) program, or, depending upon education and experience, receive a direct appointment. Dial 1-800-USA-ARMY for further recruiting information or visit their Web site at *www.army.mil*.

Join the Navy   Navy applicants may be as young as 17 years old with parental consent or otherwise be 18 to 34 years old; be U.S. citizens or legal aliens; pass the ASVAB; and meet certain fitness requirements. Because of long and extensive training requirements, the maximum enlistment age in the Navy's nuclear field is 25. Commissioning programs for navy officers are available for students still in college as well as graduates, and for specialists in certain professional, scientific, and medical fields. For recruiting information, call 1-800-USA-NAVY, or visit the Navy Web site at *www.navy.mil*.

Join the Air Force   In addition to being in good health and earning the minimum scores on the ASVAB, Air Force enlistees must be between 17 and 27 years of age. To qualify for an Air Force officer commission, you must be a U.S. citizen and hold the minimum of a bachelor's degree from an accredited college. For more information call 1-800-423-USAF or visit the Air Force Web site at *www.af.mil*.

Join the Marines   Marine enlistees must be American citizens or registered aliens, be between the ages of 17 and 29, pass the ASVAB, and be in good health. More than any other service branch, the Marines enforce strict physical, mental, and moral standards. Expect rigorous and physically demanding training. Students with musical talent may wish to explore opportunities in the Marine Corps bands or the Marine Corps Drum and Bugle Corps. For an officer commission, the Marines require applicants to be U.S. citizens at least 20 and less than 30 years of age and have (or will have) a four-year college degree at the time of service. Contact a Marine recruiter by calling 1-800-MARINES or visiting the Marines' Web site at *www.usmc.mil*.

Join the Coast Guard   The Coast Guard, part of the U.S. Department of Homeland Security and the smallest of the armed forces, may be placed under the command of the Navy in times of war. At all times the Coast Guard performs duties that ensure maritime safety. Coast Guard recruits must be between 17 and 27 years old, have a high school diploma, have no more than two dependents, be in good health, and make at least the minimum required scores on the ASVAB. Attendance at the Coast Guard Academy or Officer Candidate School may lead to a Coast Guard officer commission. Direct commissions may also be offered, depending on education and experience. For more information call 1-800-GET-USCG or visit the Coast Guard Web site at *www.uscg.mil.*

★ *ROTC Opportunities*

The Army, Navy, Air Force, and Marine Corps all offer ROTC (Reserve Officers Training Corps) programs which train qualified applicants to become officers upon graduation from college. ROTC programs provide the most common path to officer commissions. As part of the program, students take full course loads that include military science courses designed to provide them with the specialized skills a military officer needs. In addition to their scholastic obligations, ROTC candidates attend weekly military labs, drills, and other training activities.

In addition, ROTC scholarships finance hundreds of educations each year. Scholarship awards are based on merit in high school academic records, SAT or ACT scores, and extracurricular activities. While the terms and amounts of ROTC scholarships vary by service, all branches offer four-year scholarships that include full tuition, books, fees, and a monthly tax-free stipend. Some services offer health care and nurse ROTC programs and some provide three, two, and even one-year scholarships. ROTC programs are currently available in over 1,000 colleges and universities throughout the United States.

Get more ROTC information at the service branch Web sites listed above.

I N TIMES OF PEACE, trained military reservists stand waiting and ready to take action should Congress and the president issue a declaration of national emergency or war. Under the control of the Secretary of Defense, through their respective military departments, over 1.25 million reservists currently serve.

Serving in the reserves reaps its members benefits nearly identical to those serving in the active military, including eligibility to use the Montgomery GI Bill to help pay for education, job training, student loan repayment, and more. Full-time reservists receive the same pay as active duty military personnel with part-timers earning prorated pay and allowances. Most training takes place close to home, so reservists need not sacrifice their personal lives, except in times of crisis.

In peaceful times, reservists are generally obligated to put in one weekend per month and an additional two weeks service per year. However, in times of war or crisis those obligations increase. As this book goes to print, the Army—the largest reserve branch—has soldiers deployed in approximately 20 countries with over 25,000 serving in support of Operation Iraqi Freedom, Operation Enduring Freedom, and in the continental United States.

THE NATIONAL GUARD

Operating under state law as the state militia, the National Guard dates back to America's early colonial militia and our structure of government, which gives individual states independent power. The National Guard stands ready to serve its state's governor in times of statewide emergencies and disasters as well as to enforce the state's laws. Regionally based and recruited, the National Guard is under control of the state government during peacetime.

But here's the interesting part: the National Guard simultaneously serves the federal government, standing fully trained and equipped for wartime emergencies and other matters of national security. To show its appreciation, the federal government provides 90 percent of the National Guard's funding. In times of war, their respective military branches govern National Guard activities, just as if they were active forces.

GENERAL RESERVE REQUIREMENTS

- Depending on the service branch, applicants must be between the ages of 17 and 40. Check with your individual military recruiter for details on your desired reserve branch.

- You must be a U.S. citizen or registered alien.

- Applicants should be healthy and in good physical condition.

- Some military branches exclude those with certain types of previous military service.

RESERVE BRANCHES AND HOW TO CONTACT THEM

- Army Reserve   *www.armyreserve.army.mil*

- Army National Guard   *www.arng.army.mil*

- Navy Reserve   *www.navyreserve.com*

- Marine Corps Reserve   *www.marforres.usmc.mil*

- Coast Guard Reserve   *www.uscg.mil/reserve*

- Air Force Reserve   *www.afrc.af.mil*

- Air National Guard   *www.ang.af.mil*

Register with Selective Services

ALTHOUGH THE UNITED STATES converted to an all-volunteer military in 1973, men between the ages of 18 and 25 years old are still required by law to register with the Selective Service. An independent agency within the executive branch of the federal government, the Selective Service System works to provide manpower to the armed forces in times of emergency as well as to administer an alternative service program for conscientious objectors.

Almost all male U.S. citizens and non-U.S. citizens living here must register—including illegal aliens, legal permanent residents, and refugees. Men who are in the United States on student or visitor visas, or as part of a diplomatic or trade mission, are exempt.

QUICK HISTORY OF THE SELECTIVE SERVICES IN AMERICA

- **1940**   President Franklin Roosevelt signs the Selective Training and Service Act which creates the country's first peacetime draft and formally establishes the Selective Service System as an independent federal agency.

- **1948–73**   During both peace and wartime, men are drafted to fill jobs in the armed forces not filled by voluntary means.

- **1973**   The draft ends and the United States is served by an all-volunteer military.

- **1975**   Selective Service registration requirements are suspended.

- **1980**   President Jimmy Carter reinstates Selective Service registration in response to the Soviet invasion of Afghanistan.

- **Present Day**   Selective Service registration continues as a backup against underestimating the number of service personnel needed in the event of a future crisis. In 1994, President Bill Clinton declares the Selective Service a "low cost 'insurance policy' against our underestimating the maximum level of threat we expect our Armed Forces to face."

WHAT HAPPENS IN A DRAFT?

Even if the United States finds itself in a situation where more troops are needed than the current all-volunteer military can supply, it literally takes an act of Congress, approved by the president, to reinstate the draft. But if that occurs, things happen quickly as the Selective Service System must deliver the first military inductees within 193 days from the onset of a crisis.

Prior to 1971, potential draftees remained on edge the entire time they were ages 18 to 25, because qualified applicants were called to service from oldest to youngest. Under the current draft system, however, a man spends only one year in the draft's first priority category—either the calendar year he turns 20 or the year his draft deferment ends. He then moves to a lower priority category with each passing year, thereby reducing his odds of being called.

To guarantee an unbiased method of drafting men for military service, selection of those actually called to serve is based on a random matching of birth dates with priority category numbers. College students can have their inductions postponed until the end of the current semester, and seniors can postpone enrollment until the end of the academic year.

In the event of a draft, local Selective Service boards would process the potential draftees. Those who passed the military evaluation for physical, mental, and moral fitness would receive induction orders to report to a local military entrance processing station within 10 days.

CONSCIENTIOUS OBJECTORS

Conscientious objectors oppose serving in the military for religious or ethical reasons. The Selective Service Alternative Service Program attempts to match these people with local jobs deemed to make a meaningful contribution to the maintenance of the national health, safety, and interest. Length of service usually lasts 24 months—the same amount of time a man would have otherwise served in the armed forces. Alternative service jobs include health care, education, and caring for children and the elderly.

HOW TO REGISTER FOR SELECTIVE SERVICES

- You can get more detailed information as well as register for Selective Services via the Internet at *www.sss.gov*.

- You can obtain Selective Service "mail-back" registration forms at any U.S. Post Office. Simply fill out the form and mail it back to Selective Service.

- Men living overseas may register at any U.S. embassy or consular office.

- Younger men can request a Reminder Mailback Card from the Selective Service. Around the time you turn 18, you'll be sent a reminder and a simple card to fill out and send back.

- If you are applying for Federal Student Financial Aid (FAFSA), you'll find a Selective Service checkbox on the back of your application form. Simply check "Yes" on Box 29 of that form, and the Department of Education will deliver the information to the Selective Service for you.

- You can also at register at more than half the high schools in the United States. Check to see if your school has a staff member appointed as a Selective Service Registrar.

Support Our Men and Women in uniform

VOLUNTEER FOR THE USO

MANY MAY REMEMBER THE annual Bob Hope television specials—but the United Service Organization (USO) is much more. Its mission is to provide for the morale, welfare, and recreation of uniformed military personnel working in the United States and around the world as well as to deliver "a touch of home."

A nonprofit, nongovernmental agency that depends on the time and financial generosity of the American people, the USO is chartered by Congress and is endorsed by the president and the Department of Defense. In 2006, more than 25,000 USO volunteers provided an estimated 488,798 hours of service at 130 centers and mobile canteens around the world. Over 5.3 million service personnel and their families visit USO centers each year. Services offered include free Internet and e-mail access, libraries and reading rooms, housing and travel assistance, support groups, nursery facilities, game rooms, and celebrity entertainment tours. The USO also reaches out to military personnel through airport centers, and family and community centers.

If you would like to volunteer your time and skills to the USO, the Web site will help you find the USO office nearest you: *www.uso.org/locations.htm*. You can also contact the USO by phone at (703) 908-6400, and you can call 1-800-876-7469 to make a financial donation.

WRITE TO A MEMBER OF OUR TROOPS

The late syndicated columnist Abigail Van Buren, also known as "Dear Abby," used her influence for years to promote good will and cheer to the men and women of the Armed Forces during the holiday season. Each year special mailing addresses were created so Abby's loyal readers could send personal holiday greetings to military personnel around the world.

Prior to September 11, 2001, the Pentagon encouraged civic-minded civilians to reach out and show their appreciation to our men and women in uniform with personal letters. Unfortunately, security measures have curtailed many letter writing programs, so

Abby's mission has now gone digital. Patriotic Americans can send e-mail messages to our troops by visiting *https://206.37.214.123/*. The service is quick, easy, and free.

The Department of Defense also maintains a Web site that encourages citizens to support and communicate with the troops at *www.americasupportsyou.mil*.

WRITE TO A MILITARY NEWSPAPER

A great way to communicate your appreciation to our troops at large is to write a letter to the editor of a service-oriented newspaper.

- The *Army Times, Navy Times*, and *Air Force Times* all operate from the same address: 6885 Commercial Drive, Springfield, Virginia 22159.

- The *Stars & Stripes*, a daily newspaper published exclusively for U.S. military stationed overseas, can be reached at 529 14th Street NW, Suite 350, Washington, DC 20045-1301. You can also e-mail your letters to the *Stars & Stripes* editor at letters@stripes.com.

Remember Our POWs and MIAs

B Y THE END OF the Vietnam War, 2,585 American prisoners of war (POWs) remained unaccounted for—either missing in action (MIA) or killed in action with no body recovered. As of

November 5, 2007, there were still 1,766 Americans missing, but they are not forgotten. The Department of Defense spends millions annually for extensive search efforts that continue in Southeast Asia, and while several hundred cases have been identified or otherwise resolved, others are still undergoing exhaustive scientific investigation and forensic analysis.

NATIONAL LEAGUE OF FAMILIES OF AMERICAN PRISONERS AND MISSING IN SOUTHEAST ASIA

Founded in 1970, the League is a nonprofit, nonpartisan organization supported by contributions from the families of POWs and MIAs, veterans, and concerned citizens. Governed by a voting membership comprised of the wives, children, parents, and other close relatives of American POWs and MIAs, the League's sole purposes are to obtain:

- The release of all prisoners

- The fullest possible accounting for the missing

- Repatriation of all recoverable remains of those who died serving our nation during the Vietnam War

Staffed by only one full-time employee, who is helped by concerned citizen and family member volunteers, the League constantly strives to heighten public awareness of our POWs and MIAs and to draw attention to related issues. Visit their Web site to stay up to date on the latest news. You can also support League efforts by purchasing POW flags, bracelets, and other items that openly show your support for their important work. For more information, contact:

National League of Families of American Prisoners and
    Missing in Southeast Asia
1005 North Glebe Road, Suite 170
Arlington, Virginia 22201
(703) 465-7432
www.pow-miafamilies.org

POW/MIA RECOGNITION DAY

Every year the president signs a proclamation designating the third Friday in September as National POW/MIA Recognition Day. Across the country and around the world, local ceremonies take place throughout Recognition Week, culminating with the American national ceremony on Recognition Day. Participants come from all of the military branches and include former POWs, veterans associations, and MIA families as well as civilian civic groups.

On August 10, 1990, the 101st Congress passed U.S. Public Law 101-355, which requires the League of Families' POW/MIA flag to be flown on specified days at federal installations. The law officially designated the flag "as the symbol of our Nation's concern and commitment to resolving as fully as possible the fates of Americans still prisoner, missing, and unaccounted for in Southeast Asia, thus ending the uncertainty for their families and the Nation."

In a demonstration of bipartisanship in 1989, the leaderships of both houses hosted the historic installation of the only flag displayed in the U.S. Capitol Rotunda. The League of Families' POW/MIA flag stands as a constant reminder of America's deep commitment to honor those who served our nation and its responsibility to do everything possible to account for those who never returned.

- State-by-state listing of unaccounted for personnel from the Vietnam War at *www.pow-miafamilies.org/states/stateindex.html*

- Library of Congress, Federal Research Division POW and MIA information database at *http://memory.loc.gov/pow/powhome.html*

- Department of Defense Prisoner of War/Missing Personnel Office at *www.dtic.mil/dpmo*

Be an Informed Voter

BEING A GOOD AMERICAN starts at the voting booth. Voting is the most direct way citizens have of influencing their government and it's important at every level, from small local elections that affect your immediate neighborhood to federal elections that influence the entire nation.

Over 105 million Americans cast their vote for president on November 7, 2000, the closest presidential race since 1946—but this was still only about half the people who were eligible to vote in this important election. The theories about why Americans take this fundamental right for granted are endless, but you can't really complain about the job our politicians are doing if you didn't exercise your voice in the process that put them into office.

Worse than not voting at all is being an ill-informed voter. It's easy to get confused if you get all your political information from mudslinging television ads: Your ballot might inadvertently end up helping the side you oppose. With so many issues and candidates at stake, it can be time-consuming to become educated, but the stakes are high enough to merit getting the real facts from a variety of sources—including the candidates themselves. With the advent of the Internet, it's never been easier to get such a wide assortment of opinions and viewpoints on the issues and candidates you care about.

WHERE TO REGISTER TO VOTE

A voter registration application may be obtained from local election officials in your county, or through registration outreach programs sponsored by groups such as the League of Women Voters. You can also register to vote at state motor vehicle or drivers' licensing offices, state offices that provide public assistance or programs for the disabled, and at armed forces recruitment offices. Some states also offer registration opportunities at public libraries, post offices, unemployment offices, high schools, and universities. You can also access a voter registration form online that you can print, fill out, and mail. Go to *www.fec.gov/votregis/pdf/nvra.pdf*.

WHO MAY VOTE?

Registration requirements have slight variations from state to state, but all states require voters to be citizens of the United States and be at least 18 years of age. Some states do not allow convicted felons to vote, but others do, provided they have paid their debts to society. Most states also require you be of sound mental health. The online voter registration form listed above gives state-by-state details.

WHEN TO VOTE

General Election Day is the Tuesday following the first Monday of November. Federal (or national) elections are always held every even numbered year. Many state and local government offices are also elected on Election Day, some during odd numbered years and others during even numbered years, but this varies according to state and local law. State and local governments also determine the dates on which primary elections and caucuses are held.

 ### *Who Is Contributing to Your Politician's Campaign?*

If, like many Americans, you maintain a cynical view of a politician's ability to remain objective when the politician, or political party, has received significant financial contributions from special interest groups, it only makes sense to investigate and find out exactly who is supporting elected officials.

The Center for Responsive Politics, a nonpartisan, nonprofit research group based in Washington, DC, tracks money in politics, and observes its effect on elections and public policy. A combination of foundation grants and individual contributions supports the Center's computer-based research on campaign finance; they accept no contributions from businesses or labor unions. By visiting the Center's Web site, you can find out who gave how much to whom—candidates, politicians, political parties, or members of congressional committees, on the federal, state, and local levels. You can also call or write for information.

The Center for Responsible Politics
1101 14th Street NW, Suite 1030
Washington, DC 20005-5635
(202) 857-0044
www.opensecrets.org

- Contact the Federal Election Commission at 999 E Street NW, Washington, DC 20463. You can call toll-free at 1-800-424-9530; in Washington, at (202) 694-1100; or TTY for the hearing impaired at (202) 219-3336. The Web site is *www.fec.gov*.

- The Center for Voting Democracy is a nonpartisan, nonprofit organization that studies how voting systems affect participation, representation, and governance: *www.fairvote.org*.

- Project Vote-Smart, a national library of nonpartisan, factual information on over 13,000 elected offices and candidates for public office, is found at *www.vote-smart.org* or 1-888-VOTE-SMART.

Contact Your Elected Officials

YOUR REPRESENTATIVES IN GOVERNMENT are there for you, so it's important to provide them with feedback and suggestions about how you think things in America should be run. Many people feel that calling or writing politicians is a waste of time. Not true! Each call, fax, letter, or e-mail sent to an elected official is recorded. If enough people call a representative about a given issue, it can have a profound effect on the way that representative votes. After all, constituents (that means you and me) are the people who put our representatives in office. They have a vested interest in keeping the majority of us happy. So take an active part in government—speak up and let your voice be heard!

CONTACTING THE PRESIDENT, VICE PRESIDENT, FIRST SPOUSE, AND SPOUSE OF THE VICE PRESIDENT

Write to the "big guys and gals" in care of the White House.

The White House
1600 Pennsylvania Avenue NW
Washington, DC 20500
Telephone: (202) 456-1414
Fax: (202) 456-2461
Comment line for the hearing impaired: (202) 456-2121
Web site: *www.whitehouse.gov*
E-mail: comments@whitehouse.gov

CONTACTING MEMBERS OF THE HOUSE OF REPRESENTATIVES

Call the U.S. Capitol switchboard operator at (202) 224-3121 or (202) 225-1904 for TTY to get directly in touch with your congressional representative's office. In addition, you may choose to visit your representative's Web site to obtain his or her e-mail or postal address.

CONTACTING MEMBERS OF THE SENATE

Phone the U.S. Capitol switchboard at (202) 224-3121 and an operator will connect you directly with the Senate office you request. You can e-mail your senators from their individual Web sites. You can mail your senators by addressing envelopes to:

Office of Senator (Name)
United States Senate
Washington, DC 20510

To write to Senate committees, address mail to:

(Name of Committee)
United States Senate
Washington, DC 20510

ADDITIONAL INFORMATION

- Individual mailing addresses for your Senators can be found at *www.senate.gov/contacting/index.cfm*.

- "Write Your Representatives," is an easy online service from the government at *www.house.gov/writerep*.

- The listing of U.S. representatives' Web sites can be found at *www.house.gov/house/memberWWW.html*.

- Congress.org is a central location to write to elected officials and stay abreast of current legislation and issues: *www.congress.org*.

Register for a Political Party ★

A POLITICAL PARTY IS a group of people who have similar ideas about how the government should be run.

Most Americans are familiar with the Democratic and Republican parties, but it's shocking to learn how many think those are the only choices. Not true! Although the votes of all the third party candidates combined don't come close to those of the Democratic or Republican candidates in presidential elections, some third parties are gaining power, especially at the local and state levels. Former Minnesota Governor Jesse Ventura, previously of the Reform Party and now part of the Independence Party, stands as one of America's best known recent alternative party success stories. Governor Ventura is in good company—in 1860, alternative party candidate Abraham Lincoln won the presidential race and became the first Republican president.

If, like many Americans, you feel there is little difference between the current Democratic and Republican parties, perhaps one of the alternatives would better suit you. Try a fun and informative questionnaire that helps match your political views to the party that best represents them: Party Matchmaker Quiz at *www.3pc.net/matchmaker/quiz.html*.

WHY REGISTER WITH A PARTY?

Some voters prefer to remain independent and not register with a political party at all. However, depending on where you live, there may be advantages to registering with a party. Some states restrict voting in primary elections to those who have declared a party affiliation (and sometimes that party must be Democratic or Republican). Some voters get around this loophole by changing their party affiliation just to be able to vote in the primaries, then changing it back for the general election.

FIND OUT MORE ABOUT THE POLITICAL PARTIES

There are too many political parties to list here, but these are the major players:

- Democratic National Party   *www.democrats.org*

- Republican Party   *www.rnc.org*

- Libertarian Party   *www.lp.org*

- Green Party   *www.greenpartyus.org*

- Reform Party   *www.reformparty.org*

- Natural Law Party   *www.natural-law.org*

- Constitution Party   *www.constitutionparty.com*

ADDITIONAL INFORMATION

A comprehensive directory of all the U.S. political parties can be found at   *www.politics1.com/parties.htm.*

Use the Internet to Get Politically Active

THE INTERNET HAS REVOLUTIONIZED and mobilized political activists in a way that was never before possible. Gone are the days when organizations and candidates had to struggle with mimeographs and the slow speed, not to mention substantial expense, of spreading their word via the U.S. Postal Service. Today's activists can disseminate messages instantaneously and inexpensively, making Internet activism an especially effective tool for small, grassroots organizations, although large political entities are jumping on the digital bandwagon too.

If you have a computer, Internet connection, and e-mail address, you too can be an Internet activist. Do an Internet search for "action alert," and you'll come up with more organizations seeking help than you'll have time to read about. Everyone from environmental groups to the AFL-CIO, the Christian Coalition, and the National Organization for Women wants you to call, write, or e-mail your representatives, boycott certain goods and services, and otherwise exercise your power as a U.S. citizen to influence public policy.

To streamline your search for worthy causes, go to the Web sites of organizations and candidates who support the issues near and dear to your heart. Most will offer free mailing lists that keep you informed about the latest developments in their battles and advise you of what you can do to help. In many cases, you can promote your cause by simply dashing off a quick e-mail to the appropriate senator, congressperson, or corporate CEO.

ADDITIONAL INFORMATION

- **Essential Information** Founded in 1982 by Ralph Nader, Essential Information encourages citizens to become active and engaged in their communities by educating the public on important topics often neglected by the mass media and policy makers. The site includes direct links to Web activism opportunities: *www.essential.org*.

- **The American Legion** Support veterans' issues by checking out the Legion's Action Alert list at *www.capwiz.com/legion/home*.

★ Internet Activism in Action

During the 2000 presidential election, Libertarian Party candidate Harry Browne found himself ignored by the same mainstream media who consistently gave airtime to third party candidates Ralph Nader and Pat Buchanan. Ironically, Browne was on the ballot in more states than either of his third party opponents, and his Rasmussen poll numbers regularly hovered slightly below Nader's and either equal to or above Buchanan's. Yet the media consistently featured the two politicians with the biggest celebrity name recognition, while disregarding the candidate from the United States' third largest political party.

When the television program *Meet the Press* decided to do a third party candidate debate show that featured only Ralph Nader (Green Party) and Pat Buchanan (Reform Party), Browne's Libertarian Party supporters sprung into action. Because of a large and vital e-mail list, Browne's campaign managers were able to let supporters quickly know of the situation and how they could help. What followed was a barrage of phone calls that jammed the *Meet the Press* switchboards and flooded the show's e-mail boxes to the point where it couldn't be ignored. While Browne's press secretary, Jim Babka, was told it was too late to change the lineup of that particular show, the group's Web activism resulted in *Meet the Press* airing another episode featuring Harry Browne and fellow third party candidates John Hagelin (Natural Law Party) and Howard Phillips (Constitution Party).

Babka says the victory absolutely, positively wouldn't have been possible without the high speed and low cost of the Internet, and if he had it to do all over again, he would, but start even earlier. Throughout his campaign, Harry Browne and his campaign staff kept in constant contact with the Web activists, keeping them up to date with every triumph and setback and making them feel a part of the campaign process, virtually. Now that the election is over, Jim Babka still uses the Internet and e-mail to motivate and activate supporters and raise funds, this time for DownsizeDC.org, which seeks to educate the public about individual liberty, personal responsibility, and small, constitutionally limited government.

Apply for a Presidential Appointment

OK, IT'S A LONG shot for the average citizen to get a presidential appointment, but this is a free country and absolutely nothing is stopping you, me, or the guy next door from trying. In fact, you can even get the application over the Internet!

According to the White House, "one of President Bush's top priorities is to select men and women of the greatest ability and highest ethical and professional integrity to serve in policymaking and key administrative positions in his administration."

If that sounds like you, read on!

Presidential appointments are an ongoing effort. Some appointments require Senate confirmation, including positions throughout the federal government, cabinet and subcabinet positions, members of regulatory commissions, ambassadors, judges, and members of numerous advisory boards. However, the president also makes many other political appointments that do not require Senate confirmation.

THE DOWNSIDE OF BECOMING A PRESIDENTIAL APPOINTEE

To let you know what you're getting yourself into, the White House offers these warnings to potential appointee candidates:

- The hours are long and the pace intense.

- There is a lot of public and press scrutiny, as you would expect in an open, democratic form of government such as ours.

- Most applicants under serious consideration for an appointment will go through a full FBI background check in which their employment, professional, personal, travel, medical, financial, legal, military, and educational histories will be reviewed and scrutinized.

- The financial holdings and sources of income for most applicants under serious consideration must be disclosed for review for possible conflicts of interest; any conflicts must be remedied by divestiture, the creation of special trusts, and so on.

- Most appointees' dealings with the federal government during and for a period of time after their service will be significantly restricted to prevent possible conflicts of interest.

THE PROCESS

Anyone wanting to apply for a noncareer position in the executive office of the president or a federal department, agency, or commission should fill out the online application form and submit it electronically, after which you'll be sent a confirmation that your application was received. Your information will be kept on file for as long as the president is in office, and you will be considered for the position or subject area in which you have expressed an interest whenever openings occur.

If you are considered for a specific position, you'll need to fill out a Personal Data Statement for White House review detailing any possible conflicts of interest derived from your sources of income, and all aspects of your personal and professional life—in short, they'll look for anything that might embarrass the president or you if he or she should choose you for a position in their administration.

If the White House is further interested in your nomination, you will be required to fill out FBI and financial disclosure forms for subsequent review and approval. If the position for which you are being considered requires Senate confirmation, the Senate committee that reviews nominations for that position may ask you to provide even more information. Be aware that any and all information you provide during any part of this process is ultimately subject to public disclosure per the Freedom of Information Act.

ADDITIONAL INFORMATION

The White House prefers that appointment applicants apply over the Internet. For the Presidential Appointment application, go to *www.whitehouse.gov/appointments*.

If you have disabilities and are having trouble accessing the appointments application form online, contact:

Presidential Personnel Office
The White House
Washington, DC 20502
Phone: (202) 456-9713
Fax: (202) 456-1121

THERE'S NO BETTER WAY to feel like you are making a difference in our country than by getting actively involved in an election campaign. After all, you'll be fighting for the issues most important to you and the candidates you feel will best serve our country.

Winning an election is an enormous job that requires teamwork. Citizens will find endless volunteer positions available throughout the campaign. Don't worry if you don't think you have any skills, a political campaign can always find a use for an enthusiastic supporter. The closer it gets to election day, the more help is needed for last-minute campaigning to motivate voters to get to the polls. Contact your favorite candidate's or political party's local headquarters to find out what you can do to get involved.

CAMPAIGNS AS CAREERS

A successful campaign requires strategic planning, strong organization, and thorough knowledge of the latest cutting-edge techniques. If you want to pursue a career in campaigning, there are lots of educational choices to help you achieve your goals. The following schools currently offer programs in campaign management:

- The Graduate School of Political Management, The George Washington University, Washington, DC, offers an M.A. degree in the field of political management. Students may select from six areas of concentration: political leadership, issues management, campaign management, lobbying and government relations, quantitative strategies, and environmental politics.

- Center for Congressional and Presidential Studies, Campaign Management Institute at American University School of Public

Affairs, Washington, DC, has an intense two-week session on campaign management for graduate credit.

- Graduate Program in Political Campaigning, Department of Political Science, University of Florida at Gainesville, offers courses in public opinion, survey research, voting behavior, political communication, and campaign strategy and tactics.

- Political Campaign Management Institute, University Extension, University of California at Davis offers undergraduate credit for a comprehensive three- to four- day training program that includes campaign strategy, organizing, voter contact, volunteer recruitment, leadership, polling, message design, and fund-raising.

- Political Communications Center, University of Oklahoma at Norman, coordinates undergraduate, Master's, and Ph.D. degrees for students specializing in political communication.

- The Ray C. Bliss Institute of Applied Politics, University of Akron, in Akron, Ohio, offers undergraduate and graduate credit courses in the history, organization, and management of campaigns.

CAMPAIGNS & ELECTION MAGAZINE

Want to learn more about how campaigns are run without going back to college? This monthly magazine (published ten times a year) provides essential "how to" information for local, state, and federal political candidates, campaign staffs, party activists, political consultants, and interested individuals, covering the trends, strategies, and techniques of modern candidate and issue campaigning. For more information or a subscription, call (703) 778-4028 or toll-free at 1-800-771-8252. Visit their Web site at *www.campaignline.com*.

Reduce America's Oil Dependence

THE AMOUNT OF OIL we import affects not only the price we pay at the gas pump, but also our environment, our national economy, and even our national security. We can all do something to help by considering the implications of the choices we make when purchasing our vehicles. Transportation accounts for two-thirds of the total U.S. petroleum use and half of that goes to run passenger cars and light trucks.

On average, the U.S. uses over 250 billion gallons of oil and petroleum products each year. Over half of the oil we currently use must be imported, and the need to import oil has sometimes resulted in less than ideal political alliances. Because about 75 percent of the world's oil supply is concentrated in the Middle East and is controlled by the Organization of the Petroleum Exporting Countries (OPEC) oil cartel, the United States is in a vulnerable position. Price shocks and manipulation by the cartel from 1979 to 2000 cost the U.S. economy about $7 trillion, and an economic depression has followed every major OPEC price shock in the last 30 years.

BEING PATRIOTIC WITH YOUR CAR

In regard to Americans' current penchant for flying flags from their vehicles, Bill Maher, comedian and controversial television host of

HBO's *Real Time with Bill Maher* said, "You can show your patriotism on your car, or you can show it *with* your car." Maher was talking about how driving electric and hybrid vehicles that use little or no gasoline, as opposed to the oversized, gas guzzling SUVs that currently clog our roads and highways, could eliminate our dependence on foreign oil.

Hybrid cars like the Honda Civic Hybrid or the Toyota Prius, which use a combination of electric and gasoline power, can travel over 600 miles on a single tank of gas. You could also opt to forgo gasoline altogether with either a totally electric vehicle or by going biodiesel. It sounds too good to be true, but it is in fact possible to transform leftover cooking oil into fuel for your car or truck. Alternative fuel pioneers like Willie Nelson, Cheryl Crow, and Laurie David have been traveling the country in biodiesel-fueled busses to bring awareness to the tremendous potential of this clean and renewable fuel. In many cases no engine alterations are necessary to run biodiesel in a regular diesel engine, although you need to check your warranty before adding biodiesel to your vehicle.

A lot of Americans don't realize that reliable hybrid, electric, and biodiesel vehicles are not a science fiction dream of the future. They are right here, right now, and they can be as affordable as their gas-driven counterparts. Whether you opt for a hybrid, electric, biodiesel, or a fuel-efficient gasoline-powered car, choosing a vehicle that conserves petroleum products sends a clear message to auto manufacturers that consumers will support the technological advances needed to make cars even more energy efficient in the future.

PROTECT THE GLOBAL ENVIRONMENT

Our transportation choices also affect the air we breathe, the ecology of our oceans, and the warming trend of our planet. Before purchasing your next vehicle, consider these compelling facts from the Environmental Protection Agency (EPA):

- Energy-related activities are the primary sources of U.S. man-made greenhouse gas (GHG) emissions, and highway vehicles are a major source of man-made GHGs in the U.S., accounting for about 25 percent of our CO_2 emissions each year (about 1.5 billion metric tons in 2003). Driving an energy-efficient vehicle can substantially reduce CO_2 emissions. A car that gets 25 miles per gallon will produce about 17 fewer tons (260 thousand fewer cubic feet) of CO_2 per year than a car that gets only 20 miles per gallon.

- Nine million gallons of petroleum are spilled into U.S. waters in a typical year. A single major oil spill can double that amount.

- More than a third of the oil shipped by sea is destined for the United States. Using less oil will make future oil spills less likely.

- Petroleum fuels also leak from storage tanks, contaminating groundwater and streams. The EPA reports about 1,000 confirmed releases each week.

- Over 100 million Americans live in areas that failed at least one National Ambient Air Quality Standard.

- Transportation vehicles produce 25 to 75 percent of key chemicals that pollute the air, causing smog and health problems.

- All new cars must meet federal emissions standards. But as vehicles get older, the amount of pollution they produce increases. Vehicles with better fuel economy to begin with may produce less pollution over time than vehicles with lower fuel economy.

SAVE MONEY

Being fuel-economy conscious doesn't mean you have to settle for a car that doesn't meet your needs. But if you take the time to shop wisely and compare and contrast, you'll get the best car for your money that provides the features you need for the highest level of fuel economy possible. Both the environment and your wallet will thank you. According to the Department of Energy, the owner of a 30 mpg vehicle will spend $663 less annually on gasoline than the owner of a 20 mpg vehicle, assuming 15,000 miles of driving annually and a fuel cost of $2.65 per gallon. Over a five year period, the 30 mpg car will save you $3,313. This study was done some time ago, so at today's fuel prices the savings are even greater.

ADDITIONAL INFORMATION

How much oil did the United States import this month? Stay up to date with the latest statistics from the Department of Energy at *www.eia.doe.gov/emeu/ebr/ebrnoi.html*.

Sponsored by both the Department of Transportation and the Environmental Protection Agency, this informative, interactive Web site gives you the tools to make informed transportation decisions as you discover information about fuel efficiency ratings for nearly every vehicle on the consumer market. You can find and compare cars by make, class, and miles per gallon, find out which vehicles received the best and worst mpg ratings, get driving tips that will improve your car's gas mileage, and learn more about fuel economy and its global impact. A handy Web tool even lets you estimate the annual fuel costs of any car. Visit *www.fueleconomy.gov*.

Learn all about biodiesel at *www.biodiesel.org*.

Recycle, Reuse, Conserve

PROTECTING OUR NATURAL RESOURCES and environment is one of the most important duties for good Americans. Making the most of our resources conserves them for future generations, cleans up our air and water, and positively affects our national economy. As President George W. Bush, in his presidential proclamation declaring November 15, 2001, as America Recycles Day, stated:

- Buying products made of recycled materials contributes to domestic energy conservation and, ultimately, to a cleaner environment. Such items may range from recycled content paper, retread tires, and re-refined oil, to concrete and insulation containing recycled materials.

- Recycling one aluminum can saves enough energy to run a television set for three hours.

- Recycling a ton of glass saves the equivalent of nine gallons of fuel oil.

- The United States generates more than 230 million tons of

municipal solid waste every year, which amounts to 4 pounds of trash per person per day.

- Thanks to the efforts of the American people, we are now recovering more than 64 million tons of usable material annually.

- Recycling solid waste prevents the release of 37 million tons of carbon into the air—roughly the amount emitted annually by 28 million cars.

THINK GLOBALLY, ACT LOCALLY

Through partnerships of government agencies and corporate sponsors, Earth 911 gives consumers easy access to local, community-specific information that can help them recycle, conserve, and reuse, at no cost to taxpayers. Phone toll-free 1-800-CLEANUP or visit *www.earth911.org* and simply enter your ZIP code. The Internet or voice recognition system will guide you to local information about:

- Recycling center locations

- Buying recycled products

- Household hazardous waste

- Energy conservation

- Composting

- Dozens of other resources

A MERICA'S CROPS, LIVESTOCK, PETS, and environment are under constant threat of attack by a variety of animal and plant diseases. As hard as it may seem to believe, a single piece of infected fruit or meat can wreak havoc on American agriculture and have repercussions that affect everyone from farmers and ranchers to merchants and consumers.

All travelers, whether U.S. residents or not, play an important part in protecting our country's agriculture. The Animal and Plant Health Inspection Service (APHIS), run by the Department of Agriculture (USDA), requires that travelers entering the United States from a foreign country must declare all:

- Fruits

- Vegetables

- Plants and plant products of any kind

- Meat and meat products of any kind

- Animals, birds, and eggs

At certain times and ports of entry, APHIS personnel may use dogs or low-energy x-ray machines to reveal hidden agricultural products. Failure to declare any items may result in delays and fines. In addition to the written declaration on your customs form, inspectors may also ask if you have visited a farm or ranch during your foreign travels. Before you answer, keep in mind that APHIS inspectors carry the authority to search your baggage for undeclared items.

Even agricultural products of U.S. origin taken out of the country should be declared, as they are not always allowed to reenter the country. Some states may also require agricultural inspections of vehicles entering their borders.

ADDITIONAL INFORMATION

- For recorded traveler information from the U.S. government, call 1-866-SAFGUARD.

- Plant and animal quarantine lists change; to stay up to date, visit the Animal Plant and Health Inspection Service Web site at *www.aphis.usda.gov* and search for the latest quarantine information.

Safeguard America's Water Supply and Our Environment

THINK THERE'S NOT MUCH you can do to protect our nation's water supply and environment? Think again.

Thousands of private citizens throughout the country are regularly analyzing water samples, evaluating and restoring the health of streams and other aquatic biological communities, monitoring land uses that could affect water quality, and cleaning up beaches, as well as performing other important ecological and conservation jobs. The volunteer efforts, often coordinated through environmental groups, clubs, and state or local governments, have resulted in the reporting of water trends that might have otherwise remained unmonitored and unnoticed. Some of the larger organizations have as many as several thousand volunteers, but many are small grassroots efforts, often affiliated with neighborhood associations, schools, and civic clubs. The work of these concerned citizens has made a serious positive impact on our environment, resulting in increased public awareness of problems and changes in legislation that have resulted in cleaner, safer water and more environmentally sound public policy. In fact, state and local agencies use volunteer data to screen for water quality problems and make community-planning decisions.

Recognizing the importance of citizen involvement in keeping our waters safe, the U.S. Environmental Protection Agency (EPA) encourages and supports volunteer water monitoring by offering sampling method manuals for volunteers and providing technical assistance. The EPA also works to coordinate volunteer efforts by publishing a nationwide directory of volunteer programs and sponsoring national and regional conferences that encourage information exchanges between volunteer groups, government agencies, businesses, and educators. The EPA also provides some funding for volunteer efforts, usually in the form of state grants.

ADDITIONAL INFORMATION

The Environmental Protection Agency has a number of resources available for people interested in learning more about volunteer monitoring and how they can participate. Contact them through their local agencies or visit their Web site at *www.epa.gov.*

Citizens in Action: How a Bicycle Trail Is Helping Restore Blacklick Creek

Sometimes an unlikely catalyst can put the wheels of positive political and environmental change in motion. Such is the case in Western Pennsylvania, where a hiking and biking trail has stoked the fires of economic and political change needed to curb the current polluting of Blacklick Creek as well as begin healing the environmental damage left by decades of acid mine drainage.

Over 75,000 visitors annually enjoy the study in contrasts provided by the Ghost Town Trail and the adjacent 675-acre Blacklick Valley Natural Area. Along the 12-mile limestone-packed biking, hiking, and equestrian trail, wildflowers and wildlife exist hand in hand with mountains of sulphurous coal mining waste and a waterway that locals describe as "red and dead."

Cambria and Indiana Trail Council chair Laurie Lafontaine says residents were so used to their local environment being ravaged that they took it as a matter of course. "It was the trail that brought other people from outside the area in, that opened our eyes to our natural treasure right in our own backyard," says Lafontaine, who in the early 1990s founded the grassroots organization that turned an unused railroad right-of-way into the recreation area it is today.

Lafontaine's group has teamed with others, like the Blacklick Creek Watershed Association, to bring public attention to environmental problems as well as to lobby for political change. A walk or ride along the Ghost Town Trail provides visitors with a provocative glimpse into Pennsylvania's past, present, and future—forcing them to take a long hard look at the ravages humans can inflict on nature, while offering hope for the future.

For more information about visiting the trail, contact the Westsylvania Heritage Corporation at 105 Zee Plaza, Hollidaysburg, PA 16648; visit *www.westsylvania.org*; or call (814) 696-9380.

For more information about the national Rails-to-Trails Conservancy and their work converting unused former railway corridors into natural recreational playgrounds, write to Rails-to-Trails Conservancy; 1100 17th Street NW, 10th Floor, Washington, DC 20036; visit *www.railstrails.org*; or call (202) 331-9696.

Think Globally, Act Locally

SOMETIMES THE MOST EFFECTIVE way for individual citizens to change the world is to start in their own backyard. People all over America are actively initiating economic, environmental, and social improvements in their communities that have far-reaching effects for all Americans. They bring public awareness to important issues, lobby for social change, and directly impact the people in their communities who most need help.

Some organizations born of local grassroots efforts graduate to effect change on larger scales, becoming involved in local, regional, or even global activities. For example, local Los Angeles grassroots organizations that have gained national prominence include the White Lung Association, which leads the fight to ban asbestos, and the Living Wage Movement, which battles to ensure all full-time workers earn a wage at or above the federal poverty line. Other organizations like the Del Amo Action Committee, which led the fight to clean up two of the country's most toxic waste dumps, located in East Los Angeles, deal with local problems in their immediate area before they warrant national intervention.

Are there issues in your community that need attention? Chances are, if they're serious enough to have attracted your notice, there might already be a grassroots campaign underway to help fix the problem. In almost all cases, the citizens of a particular community know more about their community's challenges, strengths, and weaknesses than the politicians miles away at the state capital or in Washington, DC. Check local newspapers for reporting on the issues you feel are important in your community, read local bulletin boards (especially on college campuses), or search the Internet, especially local community sites. Because of small budgets, grassroots activists often turn to the Internet as their most important and effective communication tool.

If there is no organization that supports your cause, it just may be waiting for someone like you to rally support and fight for social and political change. An Internet search under "grassroots activism" will help you find lots of advice and support on starting your own campaigns.

☆ *Supporting Local Efforts: Change Not Charity*

What do three Los Angeles groups—the White Lung Association, the Living Wage Movement, and the Del Amo Action Committee—have in common? They, and hundreds of other local grassroots organizations, have been helped by the Liberty Hill Foundation.

Started in 1976 by four idealistic people who pooled their inherited wealth and launched the foundation with only

$69,000 and a commitment to making lasting change in people's lives, Liberty Hill has since given away more than $26.1 million to Los Angeles area community organizations. With the motto "Change Not Charity," the Liberty Hill Foundation seeks to put funding in the hands of the people most affected by social problems. Liberty Hill firmly believes these people are the most qualified to know how best to solve their own community's problems.

In a town that claims the largest number of poor of any U.S. metropolitan area as well as the highest number of high-income households, the Liberty Hill Foundation seeks to link these two opposing worlds that live within miles of each other. Since its founding, the organization has always placed an emphasis on "seed funding"—money that helps people with a good idea and a commitment to change, but little financing. Many of the Liberty Hill funded groups, while worthy causes, routinely find themselves passed over by traditional charities. Although not all of the Foundation's "start-ups" achieve success, they view their grants as "venture capital for social change." Liberty Hill's community funding boards claim to have the street smarts to recognize when a little money can make a huge impact on an important grassroots project. It's more than just an idle claim—after five years, 80 percent of these organizations are still operating.

In recognition of its expertise in funding grassroots organizations, Liberty Hill was recently awarded a pioneering $1.5 million grant by the Ford Foundation to further the cause of their unique brand of philanthropy. In addition to funding, the Liberty Hill Foundation provides training and technical assistance to organizations and works to convene activists and donors around critical issues facing local Los Angeles area communities.

To learn more about the accomplishments of this important organization or to help, visit *www.LibertyHill.org* or write to Liberty Hill Foundation, 2121 Cloverfield Boulevard, Suite 113, Santa Monica, CA 90404.

Be Smokey Bear's Friend and Help Prevent Forest Fires

SMOKEY BEAR HAS BEEN encouraging citizens to take a personal interest in preventing forest fires for well over 50 years, but many people don't realize there actually was a real Smokey Bear. During a devastating 1950s forest fire in New Mexico's Lincoln Forest, a small bear cub, in an attempt to escape the blazing inferno around him, climbed to the top of a tree. Firefighters eventually found the frightened cub, in the middle of a charred forest, perched in the blackened tree's skeleton. Moved by the animal's bravery, the firefighters christened the cub "Smokey." After nursing him back to health, the firefighters sent Smokey to live out his days in comfort at the National Zoo in Washington, DC.

The original Smokey passed away in 1976. A second Smokey was adopted, but when this bear died in 1990, the living symbol of Smokey Bear was laid to rest as well, although the bear's cartoon image remains to remind Americans that only they can prevent forest fires.

VISIT SMOKEY BEAR'S GRAVE

Visitors can pay respects at the grave of the original Smokey Bear in Capitan, New Mexico. Over 500 items of Smokey memorabilia are on display at the adjacent Smokey Bear Museum. Capitan is located in the center of historic Lincoln County, New Mexico, at the junction of U.S. Highway 380 and NM highways 48 and 246. For more information call the Smokey Bear Park and Museum at (505) 354-2748 or learn more about Smokey Bear at *www.smokeybear.com*.

CAMPFIRE SAFETY TIPS

- Be sure your fire pit has a metal fire ring; otherwise, circle the pit with rocks.

- Clear at least a 10-foot area around the pit down to the soil.

- Keep plenty of water nearby, as well as a shovel for throwing dirt on the fire.

- Be sure to stack extra firewood upwind and away from the fire.

- Check that your match is out cold after lighting the fire.

- Keep your campfires small.

- Never leave campfires unattended. Even a small breeze can cause fires to spread quickly.

- To extinguish it, drown the fire with water, ensuring all embers, coals, and sticks are wet. Be sure to move rocks, as burning embers may hide underneath. After dousing everything, stir the remains, add more water, and stir again.

- Feel all materials with your bare hand to make sure no roots are left burning.

- Do not bury burning coals, as they can smolder and break into flame.

Be Prepared for Emergencies and National Disasters

D ISASTERS HAPPEN—EARTHQUAKES, FIRES, floods, hurricanes, tornadoes, terrorist attacks. If you prepare for disasters, you'll stand a better chance of staying safe and protecting your family should you ever find yourself faced with an emergency. You'll also need less help from already overworked emergency workers who could otherwise be helping other citizens more in need. Bringing along your own supplies will ensure that your family will have what they need, leaving emergency stores available for others.

The Federal Emergency Management Administration (FEMA) provides a wealth of information to help Americans prevent emergencies when possible, and effectively cope with them when necessary. Leaving no natural disaster stone unturned, FEMA's disaster preparedness Web site can teach you what to do during earthquakes, chemical spills, sudden floods, hurricanes, tornadoes, fires, landslides, and even tidal waves and volcanic eruptions: *www.fema.gov*.

PREPARE A DISASTER SUPPLIES KIT

FEMA suggests all citizens prepare disaster supply kits filled with the essentials they might need in an emergency evacuation. You should include:

- A supply of water, one gallon per person per day. FEMA recommends storing water in sealed, unbreakable containers. Identify each water container with its storage date and replace it every six months.

- A supply of nonperishable packaged or canned food and a non-electric can opener

- A change of clothing, rain gear, and sturdy shoes

- Blankets or sleeping bags

- A first aid kit and prescription medications

- An extra pair of glasses

- A battery-powered radio and flashlight and plenty of extra batteries

- Credit cards and cash

- An extra set of car keys

- A list of family physicians

- A list of important family information, including the style and serial number of medical devices such as pacemakers

- Special items for infants, elderly, or disabled family members

The Federal Highway Administration wants to help you stay safe on the road. Their Web site can put you in touch with the latest information about weather conditions, road closings, construction reports, traffic reports, and other transit-related data: *www.fhwa.dot.gov/trafficinfo*. To stay prepared for emergencies while traveling, FEMA recommends everyone carry an emergency kit in their car that contains:

- A battery-powered radio and a flashlight, and extra batteries

- A blanket

- Booster cables

- A fire extinguisher (5-pound, A-B-C type)

- A first aid kit and manual

- Bottled water and nonperishable high-energy foods such as granola bars, raisins, and peanut butter

- Maps

- A shovel

- A tire repair kit and pump

- Flares

BIOTERRORISM PREPAREDNESS

The Centers for Disease Control (CDC) provides public health and emergency preparedness and response, with details for biological, chemical, and radiological agents and threats. The CDC also helps citizens prepare for emergencies related to diseases and health. For more information contact:

CDC Bioterrorism Preparedness and Response Program
Emergency Hotline: (770) 488-7100
Program Questions: (404) 639-0385
www.bt.cdc.gov

ENVIRONMENTAL PREPAREDNESS

The Environmental Protection Agency believes that the more you know about hazardous chemicals and other factors affecting the environment in your community the better prepared you'll be to manage these potential dangers. Citizens and activists can gather information to profile the chemicals stored and released in their communities, understand the chemical hazards posed, implement plans to prevent problems, and develop emergency plans in case of accidents. You can find lots of citizen environmental stewardship opportunities at *www.epa.gov/stewardship*. To report oil and chemical spills, call the EPA's National Response Center at 1-800-424-8802.

☆ *Learn About the Emergency Alert System*

"This is a test of the Emergency Alert System. This is only a test. . . ." We've all heard the words, but what do they really mean?

In 1994, the Emergency Alert System (EAS) replaced the

Emergency Broadcast System as the means for the president to address the American people in the event of a national emergency. Thousands of broadcast stations, cable systems, and participating satellite programmers provide access to the EAS.

Although the system has never actually been used for its intended purpose, anyone who watches television or listens to the radio is familiar with the regular tests that assure us that the system is working. All AM and FM radio stations, television broadcast stations, and cable systems that have 10,000 or more subscribers have the capability to transmit emergency messages.

The Federal Communications Commission (FCC) has a toll-free number that provides information on a wide variety of subjects, including the EAS: 1-888-CALL- FCC; the TTY number is 1-888-TELL-FCC. You can also visit the FCC Web site for further details at *www.fcc.gov.*

Help Eliminate Hunger

DESPITE THE PROSPERITY OF the United States, in 2007 more than 25 million Americans sought emergency food assistance from America's Second Harvest, the nation's largest domestic hunger relief organization. A national network of more than 200 food banks and food-rescue programs, the organization distributes donated food through 50,000 charitable agencies in all 50 states and Puerto Rico. A model of efficiency, this worthy organization manages to distribute 28 pounds of food for each dollar donated. Large corporate sponsors such as Con-Agra, Kraft Foods, Nabisco, General Mills,

Chiquita, and others help make this high ratio possible.

Children comprise about 39 percent of those helped by America's Second Harvest. Eleven percent are seniors and nearly two-thirds of adult recipients are women. The organization also fights hunger at the political level by keeping pressure on government officials about hunger-related public policy and motivating the public to do the same. Even if you can't donate dollars, following the "Action Alerts" on the Second Harvest Web site will give you lots of opportunities to join in the fight against hunger, without having to pull out your wallet: *www.secondharvest.org.*

ADDITIONAL INFORMATION

Learn about how the government, through the Department of Agriculture's Food and Nutrition Service, helps the hungry through food stamps, school lunch programs, elderly assistance, and others public programs by visiting *www.fns.usda.gov/fncs.*

Join AmeriCorps

AMERICORPS, CONSIDERED THE DOMESTIC Peace Corps, uses the services of more than 50,000 Americans in a national network of hundreds of programs throughout the United States. A few of the many available AmeriCorps jobs include tutoring and mentoring at-risk youth, building affordable homes, cleaning up rivers and streams, helping seniors to live independently, and responding to natural disasters.

Most AmeriCorps members come from and serve with projects like Habitat for Humanity, the American Red Cross, Boys and Girls Clubs of America, and a host of other local organizations and local chapters of national organizations. However, two AmeriCorps programs are managed nationally:

- *AmeriCorps VISTA (Volunteers in Service to America)* Dedicated to increasing the capability of people to improve the conditions of their own lives, VISTA volunteers live and serve full-time in the communities they help. One of VISTA's primary goals is to create social programs and change that lasts, even after the volunteer has completed their term of service.

- *AmeriCorps NCCC (National Civilian Community Corps)* A 10-month, full-time residential service program for men and women ages 18 to 24, NCCC helps meet the nation's education, public safety, and environmental needs. According to AmeriCorps, the program combines the best practices of civilian service, including leadership and team building.

QUALIFYING FOR SERVICE

An AmeriCorps term of service usually lasts from 10 months to one year, although some projects offer part-time opportunities. Other AmeriCorps eligibility requirements include:

- You must be a U.S. citizen or national, or a legal permanent resident alien.

- You must be at least 17 years old, although some service opportunities require you to be at least 18.

- AmeriCorps programs, except NCCC, carry no upper age limits.

• Some programs require specialized skills, others look for a bachelor's degree, still others require a few years of related volunteer or employment experience. For some assignments, you need nothing more than motivation and commitment.

BENEFITS OF SERVING IN AMERICORPS

• After successfully completing a year of AmeriCorps service, you will be eligible for an education award of $4,725. Part-time volunteers receive a portion of that amount.

• If you already have student loans, you can use your education award to help pay them off.

• You might be eligible for student loan deferment and forbearance if you become a full-time AmeriCorps volunteer. Your lender can tell you for sure.

• Full-time workers receive a living allowance to cover basic expenses.

• AmeriCorps will pay for the interest that is accrued on student loans for eligible members who complete their service.

• You'll gain valuable skills that can help in later careers.

ADDITIONAL INFORMATION

As AmeriCorps is a collaborative effort of many organizations, the Web site can give you the best, most comprehensive information: *www.americorps.org*.

★ SeniorCorps

SeniorCorps puts the experience and talents of older people across the country to work making valuable contributions to their communities. Civic-minded seniors may choose between three main national volunteer service programs:

- **The Retired and Senior Volunteer Program (RSVP)** makes it easy to find appealing volunteer opportunities by matching the interests and skills of older Americans with opportunities to help solve community problems. RSVP volunteers choose how, where, and how much they want to serve—from a few hours a week to a full-time job.

- **Foster Grandparents** help children with special or exceptional needs. Volunteers may work to offer emotional support to child victims of abuse and neglect, tutor kids who need extra help learning to read, mentor troubled teens, and help care for premature infants and children with disabilities and illnesses.

- **Senior Companions** help other seniors who need assistance to live independently in their own homes. Companions may help with simple chores, provide transportation, and offer friendship and companionship to those who live alone or have disabilities or terminal illnesses.

For more information about SeniorCorps volunteer opportunities, call 1-800-424-8867, or visit *www.seniorcorps.org*.

OVER THE LAST 40 years, more than 187,000 Americans have volunteered to serve their country and promote world peace and friendship by living and working in the developing world. First proposed in 1960 by then presidential candidate John F. Kennedy, the Peace Corps pursues three main goals:

- To help the people of interested countries in meeting their need for trained men and women.

- To help promote a better understanding of Americans on the part of the peoples served.

- To help promote a better understanding of other peoples on the part of Americans.

In 1961, the first Peace Corps volunteers served in six countries. At various times since, that number has grown to as many as 139 countries. As of this writing, over 7,500 Peace Corps volunteers serve in 73 developing nations around the world, helping to promote growth and progress in the following areas:

- Teaching English as a Foreign Language, the Peace Corps' largest program

- Business

- The environment

- Agriculture

- Health

- Community development

During the typical two-year Peace Corps assignment, volunteers gain many benefits beyond the satisfaction of knowing they made an important difference in the world. Highly sought-after skills such as foreign language fluency, international experience, and cross-cultural and technical training can give former Peace Corp volunteers a competitive edge in today's international job market.

PEACE CORPS VOLUNTEER REQUIREMENTS

- You must be a U.S. citizen to join the Peace Corps.

- You must be at least 18 years old to join, although there is no upper age limit. Six percent of volunteers are over 50 and the oldest volunteer currently serving is 81.

- Most assignments require a four-year college degree.

- Applicants without a college degree may qualify if they have three to five years of work experience in needed fields.

The Peace Corps provides its volunteers with transportation to and from their assignment country, comprehensive medical and dental coverage, as well as a monthly allowance to cover housing and other basic needs. Those with certain student loans may also benefit from possible deferments.

★ Prominent Peace Corps Volunteers

- If you become a Peace Corps volunteer, you'll be in good company. Here is just a small sampling of some prominent former volunteers:

- Musician, writer, and Texas gubernatorial candidate Richard "Kinky" Friedman

- Television personality Bob Vila, former host of *This Old House*

- Writer Paul Theroux, author of *The Mosquito Coast* and *The Great Railway Bazaar*

- Film director/producer Taylor Hackford (*An Officer and a Gentleman*, *The Devil's Advocate*, and *Ray*)

- Founder and CEO of Netflix, Reed Hastings

- Chicago Bears chairman of the board Michael McCaskey

- Levi Strauss chairman of the board Bob Haas

- Host of NBC's *Hardball*, Chris Matthews

- Senior editor for *People* magazine and author of *The Road to Tamazunchale*, Ron Arias

- Pulitzer Prize–winning journalist and professor Leon Dash

- Former U.S. Secretary of Health and Human Services Donna Shalala

- Executive director of the Sierra Club, Carl Pope

- Connecticut senator and presidential candidate Chris Dodd

ADDITIONAL INFORMATION

Get more information about joining the Peace Corps by calling their recruitment number, 1-800-424-8580, or by visiting the Peace Corps Web site: *www.peacecorps.gov*.

- **Peace Corps for Teens** The Peace Corps, knowing that today's youth are tomorrow's volunteers, has launched a new web site specifically designed to acquaint kids with the opportunities and rewards of volunteering for the Peace Corps: *www.peace corps.gov/ teens*.

- **Donate to the Peace Corps** Can't volunteer but want to help anyway? Donate at *www.peacecorps.gov/resources/donors/contribute*.

Help the FBI Fight Crime

A T ANY ONE TIME, the Federal Bureau of Investigation may be on the lookout for as many as 12,000 fugitives. Despite the fact that the FBI employs over 12,000 special agents and over 18,000 professional support personnel, it's no wonder they can still use some help from America's citizens.

The principal investigative arm of the United States Department of Justice, the FBI has the authority to investigate all federal criminal violations that have not been specifically assigned by Congress to another federal agency, as well as to provide cooperative services, such as fingerprint identification, laboratory examinations, and police training to other law enforcement agencies around the country. The FBI's investigative functions fall into the categories of applicant matters, civil rights, counterterrorism, foreign counterintelligence, organized crime and drugs, violent crimes and major offenders, and financial crime.

As part of the Fugitive Publicity Program, the FBI places photographs and information about fugitives in many U.S. Post Offices. More detailed and comprehensive information about ongoing investigations and individuals wanted for crimes or questioning in investigations can be found at the FBI's Web site: *www.fbi.gov.*

Ordinary citizens are encouraged to help the FBI by providing valuable tips and information; in many cases, financial rewards are offered to those who do so. You can find detailed, up-to-date information about the following types of cases at the FBI Web site:

- **Ten Most Wanted Fugitives**   Founded on March 14, 1950, by the FBI in association with the nation's news media, the Ten Most Wanted Program is designed to publicize particularly dangerous fugitives who might not otherwise receive nationwide attention. Since its inception, 150 Ten Most Wanted List fugitive apprehensions have resulted from the help of private citizens.

- **Most Wanted Terrorists**   International terrorists could be right in your back yard. Check out the photos and profiles at the FBI Web site to find out.

- **Fugitives**   You can find a month by month listing of wanted fugitives, most of whom are considered dangerous. Individuals with information concerning these cases should take no action themselves, but instead immediately contact their nearest FBI office or local law enforcement agency. For sightings outside the United States, contact the nearest U.S. embassy or consulate.

- **Kidnapping and Missing Persons**   The FBI Web site also maintains photo archives of kidnapped (including parental abductions) and missing persons so that citizens can offer valuable help or identification information. The bureau includes pertinent data about the cases, additional descriptive information about the victims and possible perpetrators, and, in some cases, age-enhanced photos of the victims so you'll know how they are likely to appear today.

- **Crime Alerts**   Crime alerts highlight certain cases and fugitives the FBI particularly needs information about.

- **Unknown Suspects**   You can browse the archives of photos, composite drawings, or security camera photos of unknown suspects caught in the act while robbing banks or committing other serious crimes and help the FBI to identify them.

- **Seeking Information**   The FBI is seeking citizens who might have information about important ongoing investigations, individuals wanted for questioning in crimes, or the identification of unidentified crime victims. Again, the Web site will give you all the details of current cases.

FIGHTING CRIME WITH RADIO AND TELEVISION

Citizens can even help the FBI by listening to the radio and watching television.

The ABC radio network program *FBI, This Week* is picked up on more than 3,200 affiliated radio stations via satellite each week. In addition to educating listeners about the Ten Most Wanted Fugitives, it gives a behind-the-scenes look at how the Bureau investigates a variety of cases from computer crime to terrorism, organized crime, and everything in between. Call your local ABC radio affiliate for broadcast times in your area. You can listen to past broadcasts online at *www.fbi.gov/thisweek/archive/radarchive.htm*.

The FBI has also utilized the power of television since 1988 on the Fox Network's *America's Most Wanted* (now known as *America's Most Wanted: America Fights Back*). Host John Walsh is a nationally known advocate for missing and exploited children who turned his own grief over the tragic abduction and death of his son Adam in 1981 into a crusade to protect children and get violent criminals off the streets. As this book goes to press, *America's Most Wanted* has resulted in the capture of 966 fugitives from justice. Because of its flexible format, the show is able to allow law enforcement officials to appeal to the public for leads concerning recently committed crimes. Time can be a crucial element in solving cases. For more information, check your local television listings or visit *www.amw.com*.

Use the Freedom of Information Act (FOIA) and the Privacy Act

THE FREEDOM OF INFORMATION Act (FOIA), enacted in 1966, gives the American people the right to access records in the possession of agencies and departments of the executive branch of the U.S. government. The form in which records are maintained does not affect their availability—requesters may seek printed documents, audio or videotape recordings, maps, photographs, computer disks and printouts, or other items.

Before this law was enacted, individuals were required to establish a right to examine government records and they had no judicial recourse if they were denied access. Things have changed, and today it's the government who must demonstrate the need for secrecy in order not to disclose documents to the public.

THE PRIVACY ACT OF 1974

The Privacy Act regulates federal government agency record keeping and disclosure practices, allowing most individuals to access federal agency records about themselves. It also restricts the disclosure of personally identifiable information by federal agents and prohibits the government from using information gathered for one purpose from being used for another purpose.

The Privacy Act stipulates that personal information in federal agency files must be accurate, complete, relevant, and timely, and gives the subject of a record the right to challenge the accuracy of the information in his or her own files. In order to ensure that federal agencies can't keep secret records, the act requires each agency to publish a full description of each system of records they maintain containing personal information.

EXCEPTIONS TO THE RULES

Neither the FOIA nor the Privacy Act guarantees absolute rights to examine all government documents, but both laws do establish a person's right to request records and to receive a response to that request, as well as the right to appeal and challenge access denials in court.

The Privacy Act maintains two general exemptions:

- All records maintained by the Central Intelligence Agency.

- Selected records dealing with criminal investigations, maintained by law enforcement agencies.

The FOIA's nine statutory exemptions protect against disclosure of information that would jeopardize national defense or foreign policy, privacy of individuals, proprietary interests of business, the functioning of the government, and other important interests.

When a record contains some information that qualifies it as being exempt, it doesn't necessarily exempt the entire record, as the FOIA specifically provides that "any reasonably segregable portions of a record must be provided to a requester after the deletion of the portions that are exempt."

THE NINE FOIA EXEMPTIONS

- *Classified documents*   Information may be classified in the interest of national defense or foreign policy.

- *Internal personnel rules and practices*   Covers matters related solely to an agency's internal personnel rules and practices.

- *Information exempt under other laws*   To qualify under this exemption, a statute must require that matters be withheld from the public in such a manner as to leave no discretion to the agency or establish particular criteria for withholding information or particular types of information.

- *Confidential business information*   This exemption also covers trade secrets and general information that could otherwise harm a business.

- *Internal government communications*   Exempting internal communications encourages productive discussion of policy matters between agency officials by allowing them to be kept from public scrutiny before their final adoption.

- *Personal privacy*   Protects the privacy of individuals by withholding information from personnel, medical, and other files that would constitute an unwarranted invasion of personal privacy.

- *Law enforcement*   Allows agencies to withhold documents that might interfere with the law enforcement process.

- *Financial institutions*   Exempts information contained in or related to examination, operating, or condition reports prepared by or for a bank supervisory agency such as the Federal Deposit Insurance Corporation, the Federal Reserve, or similar agencies.

- *Geological information*   Rarely used, the ninth exemption deals with geological and geophysical data, and maps about wells.

HOW TO REQUEST FOIA INFORMATION

- The first step in making a request under the FOIA is to identify the agency that houses the records you want. If you don't know which agency to contact, consult a government directory for a list of federal agencies and their functions.

- Most Agencies require FOIA requests be made in writing. Relax—you don't need to draft a complex legal document, just a short, simple written request. State your name and address, tell the agency your request is being made under the Freedom of Information Act, and request the records you seek as specifically as possible. This last point is important—different agencies keep different records in different ways, so the more information you can give, the more likely you'll find what you're looking for. It's often a good idea to also include your telephone number, so an agency worker can contact you if more details are needed. Since fees are sometimes charged to cover FOIA services, it's a good idea to ask about them in advance. To save yourself some time, a common practice is to include a request to be notified in advance if the fees will exceed a fixed amount.

- Address your letter to the agency's FOIA Officer or to the head of the agency. Mark the envelope containing the written request "Freedom of Information Act Request" in the bottom left corner. Always keep a copy of your request letter and any related correspondence until your request has been completely resolved.

ADDITIONAL INFORMATION

Consult the Complete Citizens Guide to Using the Freedom of Information Act at *www.sba.gov/aboutsba/sbaprograms/foia/index.html*.

Help Airport Security

THE TYPICAL AMERICAN AIRPORT experience has been forever altered since the tragic events of September 11, 2001. Gone are the carefree days of last-minute arrivals, loose carry-on baggage rules, and packing anything and everything but the kitchen sink.

Heightened airport security measures increase the time needed to check in and the Federal Aviation Administration (FAA) recommends arriving at the airport two hours before your flight's scheduled departure, earlier if you're traveling with children or persons with disabilities. By properly preparing for your trip and packing safely and wisely, you not only help our airports and skies stay secure, you help cut down the lines and wait times we all have to endure.

Adult passengers must bring a government-issued photo ID, such as a driver's license, draft card, or passport. Since required ID can vary by destination, make sure you check the requirements for your specific travel plans. The name on your ID must match the name on your airline ticket. Before leaving for the airport, use the following Transportation Security Administration (TSA) checklist to make sure you don't have any of the following banned items on your person or in your carry-on luggage:

- Except for plastic or round-bladed butter knives, knives of any length or description, including pocketknives, carpet knives and box cutters, straight razors, and ice picks. Plastic or metal blunt-tip scissors, or metal pointed-tip scissors shorter than four inches are okay.

- For the most part flammable materials like paints, lighter fluids, gasoline, and other fuels are prohibited, although small cigarette lighters are once again allowed on board after a temporary ban. Safety matches and lighters may only be carried on your person, not in checked luggage. "Strike-anywhere" matches are not permitted at all.

- Corkscrews.

- Athletic equipment that could be used as a weapon, such as baseball or softball bats, golf clubs, pool cues, ski poles, and hockey sticks.

- Fireworks, including signal flares, sparklers, or other explosives.

- Household items such as drain cleaners and solvents, chlorine bleach, and other disabling chemicals.

- Pressure containers, including spray cans, butane fuel, scuba tanks, propane tanks, CO_2 cartridges, and self-inflating rafts. Aerosol bottles and cans of hair spray and cosmetic items are allowed, if under 3 ounces.

- Weapons, including firearms, ammunition, gunpowder, mace, tear gas, or pepper spray. Unloaded firearms may be transported in checked baggage if declared to the agent at check in and packed in a suitable container. Handguns must be in a locked container. Boxed small arms ammunition for personal use may be transported in checked luggage. Allowed amounts may vary depending on the airline.

- Other hazardous materials such as dry ice, gasoline-powered tools, wet-cell batteries, camping equipment with fuel, radioactive materials (except limited quantities), poisons, and infectious substances. (Dry ice—4 pounds or less—for packing perishables, may be carried on board an aircraft provided the package is vented.)

- You may take liquids or gels—no more than 3 ounces of each—in individual containers all packed in a quart-size zip-top clear plastic bag. One zip-top bag per person is permitted.

Here are some other tips for airline travel:

- Beware—many common items used every day in the home or workplace may seem harmless, but when transported by air, they can be very dangerous. In-flight variations in temperature and pressure can cause items to leak, generate toxic fumes, or start a fire. Beware of personal care items containing hazardous materials (such as flammable perfume and aerosols).

- Electric wheelchairs must be transported in accordance with airline requirements. The battery may need to be disconnected, removed, and the terminals insulated to prevent short circuits.

- Leave gifts unwrapped. Airline security personnel will open gifts if the x-ray scan cannot determine the contents.

ADDITIONAL INFORMATION

- For more detailed information, rules, and regulations, write the Transportation Security Administration at 601 South 12th Street, Arlington, VA 22202-4220, or visit *www.tsa.gov*.

- Customs Information—Know Before You Go. Visit *www.customs.treas.gov/xp/cgov/travel* for the latest traveler's information and alerts.

THE INTRICACIES OF U.S. immigration law represent far too complex a subject for us to delve into in detail here, and the requirements are changing all the time. But generally speaking, most adults who seek naturalization must meet the following requirements:

- Be a lawful permanent resident of the United States ("green card" holder).

- Have a period of continuous residence and physical presence in the United States, usually at least five years prior to filing a naturalization application with no single absence from the United States of more than one year.

- Residence in a state or district for at least three months prior to filing.

- The ability to read, write, and speak basic English.

- Demonstration of a basic knowledge and understanding of U.S. history and government.

- Be of good moral character.

- Be willing to swear the Oath of Allegiance to the United States (known as "attachment to the Constitution"), and demonstrate a favorable disposition toward the United States.

While all citizenship applicants must show good moral character, attachment to the Constitution, and favorable disposition toward the United States, other naturalization requirements may be modified or eliminated under certain conditions. Check with your local office of U.S. Citizenship and Immigration Services (USCIS) for more details.

IMMIGRATING TO THE UNITED STATES

Before you can become a naturalized U.S. citizen, you must be a lawful permanent resident. As with all things immigration-related, millions of exceptions and loopholes to the rules exist, but most adults who immigrate to the United States will get here in one of the following three ways:

Family   Family connections provide the most common path to immigration. While family reunification is a primary goal of the USCIS, immigrating through family can nonetheless be a complex and challenging proposition. Sponsor relatives who live in the United States have significant obligations, especially financial obligations, to meet before they can bring family members here, and those relations must also meet specific qualifications. If you are a lawful permanent resident (green card holder) you may petition for your husband or wife and your unmarried children to immigrate to the United States. If you are currently a U.S. citizen and over 21 years old, your sponsorship options grow, as you are eligible to sponsor your husband or wife, unmarried or married children of any age, brothers and sisters, and parents. Expect to have to prove your immigration status, your relationship to the relative(s) you are sponsoring, and that you can support your family at 125 percent above the mandated poverty line. This last point often presents the biggest obstacle for many immigrant families.

Employment   The American immigration system's secondary goal is to allow U.S. employers to hire citizens of other countries when no qualified U.S. citizens or legal residents can fill the positions. Each year, a minimum of 140,000 employment-based immigrant visas are available in five preference categories. In most cases, aliens will need a solid offer of employment from a qualified employer who is willing, able, and qualified to sponsor them for immigration. In addition to filing the necessary forms and guaranteeing employment, the employer should also be prepared to show evidence that no qualified U.S. citizens or lawful permanent residents are available to fill the position. In the event that you can offer extensive documentation showing sustained national or international acclaim and recognition as a person of extraordinary ability in the sciences, arts, education, business, or athletics, you won't be required to have a specific job offer or a sponsoring employer to immigrate to the United States—provided you're coming here to continue work in your established field. Keep in mind this classification is reserved for those with truly extraordinary achievement, for instance Nobel prize winners.

Asylum   Potential immigrants may seek asylum by demonstrating to the United States government that they fear persecution based on race, religion, nationality, membership in a social group, or political opinion. Proving you belong in one of these protected categories can be tricky, as the legal definitions of persecution are vague at best. It is strongly recommended you seek the advice of a qualified immigration attorney in asylum cases. In a normal asylum procedure, when the applicant is already in the United States (or at a U.S. border or airport), USCIS asylum officers have the authority to grant asylum based on a first interview. If, however, you are unable to convince the asylum officer you have a valid fear of persecution and your application is denied, you will then have a chance to go in front of an immigration judge to again try to prove your case. If the immigration judge denies your application, you still have the right to further appeal your case. The entire asylum procedure must be completed within 180 days of filing the asylum application.

ADDITIONAL INFORMATION

When you speak of immigration, you may think of the Immigration and Naturalization Service (INS). But this government entity ceased to exist back in 2003 when the duties of the INS transitioned into the Department of Homeland Security (DHS). The resulting entity—U.S. Citizenship and Immigration Services—is now responsible for the administration of immigration and naturalization adjudication functions and establishing immigration services policies and priorities. Get more details about all things immigration at their Web site: *www.uscis.gov.*

Volunteer

NO MATTER WHAT YOUR age, talents, interests, or skills, you can help America become a better place by becoming a volunteer. The possibilities are literally endless. Americans have a long history of volunteering, and there's no better way to feel like you're making a difference than to help someone less fortunate or to further a cause you believe in.

If you don't think there's anything you can do to volunteer, think again. Thousands of worthy organizations and causes need your help now, including countless U.S. government entities. Here are just a few examples of federal volunteer programs where you can make a difference:

- Help our veterans through the Bureau of Veterans Affairs. Visit *www.va.gov/volunteer* or write V.A. Central Voluntary Service, 810 Vermont Avenue NW, Washington, DC 20420; or call (202) 273-8952.

- Support our National Museum by volunteering at the Smithsonian. Visit *www.si.edu/resource/faq/volunteer/start.htm* to get detailed information about all the volunteer programs available, or call Smithsonian Information at (202) 633-1000 for voice connection, or (202) 357-1729 for TTY connection.

- Volunteer for science projects that help manage resources and protect the environment at the U.S. Geological Survey. Visit *www.usgs.gov/volunteer* or write U.S. Geological Survey, 601 National Center, Reston, VA 20192.

- Protect our natural resources by working with the Natural Resources Conservation Service's Earth Team. Visit *www.nrcs.usda.gov/feature/volunteers*, or call 1-888-526-3227 or (515) 289-0325, or write to USDA-NRCS, 5140 Park Avenue Suite C, Des Moines, IA 50321.

- Help new businesses grow by volunteering for SCORE (Service Corps of Retired Executives). Call toll-free 1-800-634-0245 or visit *www.score.org*.

VOLUNTEER VACATIONS

You can have a wonderful low- or no-cost vacation while you help America by volunteering at one of our national parks, forests, or monuments. You'll be taking advantage of some of the country's most beautiful settings and scenery while helping to preserve them for future generations. Positions range from campground hosts to trail maintenance, planting trees, and other miscellaneous duties. For more information on volunteer opportunities contact:

- The Bureau of Land Management—Office of Public Affairs, 1849 C Street, Room 406-LS, Washington, DC 20240; (202) 452-5125; *www.blm.gov*

- US Army Corps of Engineers' Volunteer Clearinghouse, P.O. Box 1070, Nashville, TN 37202; 1-800-865-8337; *www.orn.usace.army.mil/volunteer*

ADDITIONAL INFORMATION

Comprehensive listing of federal and national volunteer opportunities to suit all tastes, ages, and experience levels: *www.hud.gov/volunteering/index.cfm*.

Volunteer Match Web site with the motto of "Get Out, Do Good," lists over 30,000 volunteer opportunities for just about anything you'd like to do: *www.volunteermatch.org*.

Youth Services Organization, an alliance of 200+ organizations committed to increasing the quantity and quality of opportunities for young Americans to serve locally, nationally, or globally. Write, call, or click: Youth Services Organization, 1101 15th Street, Suite 200, Washington DC, 20005; (202) 296-2992; *www.ysa.org*.

Virtual Volunteering. Volunteer from home or office with this listing of volunteer opportunities that can be completed with a computer over the Internet: *www.serviceleader.org*.

BE INFORMED

Learn about the Constitution

We the People of the United States, in Order to form a more perfect Union, establish Justice, insure domestic Tranquility, provide for the common defense, promote the general Welfare, and secure the Blessings of Liberty to ourselves and our Posterity, do ordain and establish this Constitution for the United States of America.

SO BEGINS OUR COUNTRY'S most important document, signed into power on September 17, 1787, by the delegates to the Constitutional Convention. While a lot of folks like to spout off at the mouth about what is and isn't "constitutional," many have never actually even read the document. The Constitution is brilliant and basic, constituting the essential "rule book" of how our new nation was expected to operate.

KEY POINTS OF THE CONSTITUTION

Popular Sovereignty   The United States is a government by the people, for the people. The ultimate political authority resides not in the government or in any single government official, but rather in the people. The governed retain the inalienable right to alter or abolish their government or amend their Constitution.

Rule of Law   Our government is guided by a set of laws rather than by any individual or group entity. Designed to protect individual rights and liberties, the rule of law calls for both individuals and the government to submit to the law's supremacy. In other words, the government is as accountable to the law as any individual.

Separation of Powers/System of Checks and Balances   The founding fathers sought to ensure that no one branch of government grows powerful enough to dominate over the others. Allocating governmental authority among three separate branches also prevents the federal government from growing so strong as to overpower individual state governments. While the separation of powers between the executive, legislative, and judicial branches is one of the basic doctrines in the Constitution, there are many instances where governmental powers and responsibilities intentionally overlap. For this reason the founding fathers enacted an elaborate system of checks and balances. For instance, while the president has the power to appoint federal judges, ambassadors, and other high government officials, those appointments must be confirmed by the Senate. Congress enacts laws, but the president has the power to veto them. The Supreme Court retains the right to call the activities of either of the branches unconstitutional.

Federalism   Another important component to the system of checks and balances is the system of federalism—meaning power is shared between the national government and the individual state governments, thereby limiting the national government's authority.

Judicial Review   The judicial right to hold laws unconstitutional actually predates the passage of the Constitution as some Colonial judges were known to have invalidated state laws on the grounds that they violated a state constitutional provision. Although the

Constitution contains no specific reference to the power of the Supreme Court to check abuses of the legislative and executive branches, by the early 1800s, the court had been called upon to review the constitutionality of both federal and state laws and acts, making it the chief interpreter and arbiter of the Constitution.

A QUICK OVERVIEW OF THE ARTICLES OF THE CONSTITUTION

Article I   Established the legislative branch of government—the House of Representatives and Senate—as well as provided rules for how they were to be elected and what were their duties and the limits of their legislative power.

Article II   Established the presidency, the requirements for holding the office, details of how the president is to be elected, and the scope of presidential power, including the impeachment process.

Article III   Established the judiciary segment of government with the forming of the Supreme Court and the defining of judiciary powers, including matters of treason.

Article IV   Dealt with matters of the individual states, including the admission of states, the government's guarantee to states, and privileges, immunities, and extradition among the states.

Article V   Established the process for amending the Constitution.

Article VI   Outlined the legal status of the Constitution, including debts incurred before the adoption of the Constitution, the law of the land, and the oath of service that binds legislators, executives, and judicial officers of the United States.

Article VII   Simply stated that the ratification of the conventions of nine states would be sufficient for the establishment of the Constitution between those states.

★ Visiting Independence Hall

Located in downtown Philadelphia, Independence National Historical Park spans approximately 45 acres and includes about 20 buildings open to the public. Visitors can tour Independence Hall where both the Declaration of Independence and the U.S. Constitution were created as well as view the Liberty Bell and learn about the teachings of Founding Father Benjamin Franklin. The park is open every day 9:00 a.m. to 5:00 p.m., and hours for some buildings are extended on weekends in the spring and throughout the week during July and August. Some buildings may be closed on New Year's Day, Thanksgiving, and Christmas. For more information write Independence National Historical Park, 313 Walnut Street, Philadelphia, PA 19106; call (215) 597-8974 or TTY (215) 597-1785. Visit the site at *www.nps.gov/inde*.

ADDITIONAL INFORMATION

- National Archives and Record Administration Web site about the Constitution and its history, including the full text of the Constitution: *www.archives.gov/national-archives-experience/ charters/ constitution.html*.

- National Constitution Center, established to increase awareness and understanding of the U.S. Constitution, the Constitution's history, and the Constitution's relevance to our daily lives: *www.constitutioncenter.org.*

- The Constitution for Kids, at *www.constitutioncenter.org/explore/ forkids/index.shtml.*

Learn About the Constitutional Amendments

WHILE THE MAIN BODY of the Constitution has remained unchanged since its adoption, the amendments serve as the government's way of keeping up with the times. Article V of the main document offers two ways to propose amendments to the Constitution:

- By a two-thirds vote of both houses of Congress.

- Two-thirds of the state legislatures can ask Congress to call a national convention to propose amendments. However, up to this point in our history, this method has never actually been put into practice.

Before it becomes part of the Constitution, an amendment must be ratified by three-fourths of the state legislatures. In theory, an amendment can also be ratified by special ratifying conventions in three-fourths of the states, although this method has only been used one time—to ratify the 21st amendment, which repealed prohibition.

Our Constitution was no sooner ratified than people started talking about how to improve it. Many citizens of 1789 were concerned about protecting certain freedoms and rights that the original document neglected to mention. So, on December 15, 1791, the first 10 amendments—also known as the Bill of Rights—were added to the United States Constitution:

First Amendment　Guarantees the rights of freedom of speech, religion, press, peaceable assembly, and to petition the government for a redress of grievances.

Second Amendment　Guarantees the right to keep and bear arms, albeit subject to certain regulations.

Third Amendment　States that the government is not allowed to house soldiers in private homes during peacetime without the homeowner's permission.

Fourth Amendment　Prohibits the government from searching or seizing a person's property without a warrant.

Fifth Amendment　States that a person cannot be tried twice for the same crime and cannot be compelled to testify against him or herself.

Sixth Amendment　Gives a person charged with a crime the right to a fair trial with adequate legal representation.

Seventh Amendment　Guarantees a trial by jury in most cases.

Eighth Amendment   Prohibits excessive or unusual fines or cruel and unusual punishment.

Ninth Amendment   States that the people have rights other than those specifically mentioned in the Constitution.

Tenth Amendment   States that any power not given to the federal government by the Constitution is a power either of the state or of the people.

MORE AMENDMENTS

Of all the thousands of amendment proposals put before Congress, only 33 managed to obtain the necessary two-thirds approval vote. Of those 33, only 27 constitutional amendments have passed. Here are the rest of our constitutional amendments in a nutshell:

Eleventh Amendment   Prevents citizens of a state or foreign country from suing another state in federal court.

Twelfth Amendment   Gives the president and vice president separate ballots in the Electoral College system. Prior to the adoption of this amendment, the candidate with the most electoral votes became the president and the candidate with the second highest number of votes became the vice president. (As can be imagined, this resulted in some strained and under-productive political pairings.)

Thirteenth Amendment   Ended slavery in the United States.

Fourteenth Amendment Guarantees the citizenship of all people born or naturalized in the United States, guarantees the validity of public debt, and deals with the apportionment of representatives by a given state's population.

Fifteenth Amendment Guarantees the right to vote to blacks and former slaves.

Sixteenth Amendment Gives Congress the right to collect a federal income tax, without apportionment among the States.

Seventeenth Amendment Guarantees the people the right to elect senators directly and sets forth rules for Senate terms as well as procedure for filling Senate vacancies mid-term.

Eighteenth Amendment Made it illegal to produce or sell liquor in the United States.

Nineteenth Amendment Guarantees women the right to vote.

Twentieth Amendment Changed the date the president takes office from March to January, and set forth requirements for Senate assembly.

Twenty-first Amendment Just because it was in the Constitution, didn't mean it was a good idea—the 21st amendment repealed the 18th amendment, or prohibition.

Twenty-second Amendment Established a two-term limit for the president.

Twenty-third Amendment   Gives residents of the District of Columbia the right to vote in presidential and vice presidential elections.

Twenty-fourth Amendment   Guarantees citizens the right to vote for president, vice president, and members of Congress without having to pay a voting tax.

Twenty-fifth Amendment   Gives the vice president power to assume the role of president if the president dies, becomes disabled, or resigns.

Twenty-sixth Amendment   Gives the right to vote to citizens who are at least 18 years old.

Twenty-seventh Amendment   States that no law that changes the salary of senators or representatives can take effect until an election of representatives has a chance to intervene.

ADDITIONAL INFORMATION

- Read the full text of the Bill of Rights as well as more about its history at *www.archives.gov/national-archives-experience/charters/bill_of_rights.html*.

- Read the full text of the remaining ratified amendments at *www.archives.gov/national-archives-experience/charters/constitution_amendments_11-27.html*.

- Curious about non-ratified amendments? Read about the ones that didn't make the cut at *www.house.gov/house/Constitution/Amendnotrat.html*.

Learn How Laws Are Enacted

NEW FEDERAL LAWS MAY be initiated in either the Senate or the House of Representatives. In fact, Congress spends the vast majority of its time on this very activity. The procedure of getting a law passed may seem complex, but it's all part of the system of checks and balances designed to keep our country fair and democratic.

1. The process begins when a senator or representative introduces a bill that he or she wants to become law—the exception being that only representatives are allowed to introduce tax or budget bills (sorry, senators). Of course, long before the bill is introduced, citizen activists and political lobbies have usually been hard at work to gain support for the cause and to bring the issue to their representative's attention.

2. The House clerk assigns the bill a legislative number (and letters). Bills introduced in the House of Representatives carry the letters "H.R." as part of their identification; bills introduced in the Senate carry the letter "S."

3. The Government Printing Office then prints and distributes the bills to each representative.

4. Once the bill is introduced, the Speaker of the House assigns the bill to a committee. The standing committee (or often a subcommittee) scrutinizes the bill and its implications. In the process, they hear testimony from experts and people both in favor of and opposed. The committee may then:

- *Release the bill with a recommendation to pass it on without changes.*

- *Revise, rewrite, or amend the bill before releasing it.*

- *Table it indefinitely so that the House cannot vote on it. When the Senate or House agrees to a tabling motion, the measure that has been tabled can be effectively considered defeated.*

5. If the bill is released, it's put on the calendar—a list of bills awaiting action—to await further debate and possible amendments in its house of Congress. If the bill passes by a simple majority vote, it can then move on to the other house of Congress.

6. The process now begins again as the second house debates the bill's merits and faults. If the second house feels the need to amend the bill, it must then travel back to the first house for approval of those amendments. The circle continues until both sides agree. A conference committee, made up of members from each house, usually irons out the differences between the House and Senate versions. Once approved, the printing office—in a process called enrolling—prints out the final official version, which is certified by the clerk from the introducing house.

7. The "enrolled" bill is signed by the Speaker of the House, followed by the vice president before making its way to the president for final approval. From here, four things can happen:

- *The president signs the bill and it becomes law.*

- *The president elects to veto the bill and it does not become law— although Congress can override the president's veto with a two-thirds vote of both houses.*

- *The president does nothing for 10 days. If Congress is still in session, the bill automatically becomes law.*

- *The president does nothing for 10 days. If Congress adjourns within that time, the bill does* not *become law.*

ADDITIONAL INFORMATION

- For a full, detailed, albeit academic, report on how laws are made, visit this page to read Senate Document 105–14: *http://thomas.loc.gov/home/enactment/enactlawtoc.html.*

- To stay abreast of legislation currently on the floor, visit the House of Representatives and Senate Web sites: *www.house.gov* and *www.senate.gov.*

Learn the Chain of Command of the United States

WHAT IF THE UNTHINKABLE happened and the president of the United States should die, become incapacitated, or otherwise be unable to finish his or her term in office? Most Americans know the easy answer: the vice president would take over.

It's true the 20th and 25th amendments to the Constitution establish procedures and requirements for the vice president to assume the duties and powers of the president should he or she become permanently or temporarily disabled. But what if something happened to the vice president too? Our government has a plan in place for such unlikely emergencies. Harry S. Truman signed the Presidential Succession Act of 1947 into law on July 18, 1947. Amended over the years as new cabinet positions have been added, the current law establishes presidential succession as follows:

> Vice President
> Speaker of the House
> President pro tempore of the Senate
> Secretary of State
> Secretary of the Treasury
> Secretary of Defense
> Attorney General
> Secretary of the Interior
> Secretary of Agriculture
> Secretary of Commerce
> Secretary of Labor
> Secretary of Health and Human Services
> Secretary of Housing and Urban Development
> Secretary of Transportation
> Secretary of Energy

Secretary of Education
Secretary of Veterans Affairs
Secretary of Homeland Security

WHAT IF THE OFFICE OF VICE PRESIDENT BECOMES VACATED?

What happens if the vice president leaves office during a presidential term? The 25th amendment states that the president must nominate a new vice president, who must be confirmed by a majority vote of both houses of Congress. The process was really put to the test when vice president Spiro Agnew resigned in 1973 and president Richard Nixon nominated Gerald Ford to replace him. When Nixon resigned in 1974, Ford became president. He in turn nominated Nelson Rockefeller to fill his former post.

☆ *The Presidential Cabinet*

The 15 secretaries of the independent executive departments make up the president's cabinet. In addition to fulfilling important roles in the presidential succession order, the vice president and 15 secretaries stand ready to advise the president on their respective areas of expertise. While the Constitution makes no specific mention of the cabinet, it does provide that the president may ask opinions, in writing, from the principal officer in each of the executive departments. Presidents hand-pick their cabinet members, although the Senate must approve those choices.

- Learn how the Presidential Succession Act of 1947 came to pass; search for "presidential succession" at *www.senate.gov*.

- Learn how the 25th amendment affects presidential succession; visit *http://caselaw.lp.findlaw.com/data/constitution/amendment25*.

Understand How the United States Government is Structured

OUR FOUNDING FATHERS HAD their work cut out for them—to structure a sound, strong central government while simultaneously ensuring that no individual or group within that government could ever become too powerful. The solution came in the form of a structure of three separate governmental branches, each with its own distinct powers. Not only did this divide the duties and responsibilities within the federal government, but it kept the federal government from ever gaining enough power to overthrow the will of the individual states.

Although each government branch operates independently of the others, they are all required to interact, thus creating an elaborate system of checks and balances that prevents the buildup of a concentration of power in any one area. For instance, Congress can impeach the president and federal court justices and judges; the president can veto bills passed by Congress; and the Supreme Court can declare congressional laws or presidential actions unconstitutional.

The President The leader of the country and commander in chief of the military is responsible for directing the federal government and enforcing federal laws and treaties, conducting foreign policy, approving or vetoing bills passed by Congress, advising Congress on the needs of the nation, and when appropriate, pardoning people found guilty of breaking federal law. The president must be a natural born citizen of the United States, be at least 35 years old by the time he or she will serve, and have lived in the United States at least 14 years.

The Vice President The vice president presides over the senate and casts the deciding vote in cases of a tie. He or she also must stand ready to assume the duties of president should the current president die, become disabled, or otherwise be unable to serve. The vice presidential office carries the same age, citizenship, and residency requirements as the president.

The Executive Departments The heads of the executive departments, usually called "secretaries," make up the president's cabinet and advise him or her on policy issues and how to best implement them. Fifteen departments currently help in carrying out government policies that affect nearly every aspect of our daily lives: the Department of State, the Department of the Treasury, the Department of Defense, the Department of Justice, the Department of Homeland Security, the Department of the Interior, the Department of Agriculture, the Department of Commerce, the Department of Labor, the Department of Health and Human Services, the Department of Housing and Urban Development, the Department of Transportation, the Department of Education, the Department of Energy, and the Department of Veterans Affairs.

The Independent Agencies   Executive branch independent agencies are designed to serve very specific and sometimes temporary needs. Examples include the Federal Emergency Management Agency, the Commission on Civil Rights, the Environmental Protection Agency, the Federal Trade Commission, and the United States Postal Service.

THE LEGISLATIVE BRANCH

The Senate   Made up of two senators from each state, the Senate is responsible for determining guilt or innocence in impeachment cases, confirming presidential appointments, and ratifying treaties between the United States and foreign governments. Senate members, each of whom represents the whole of their state, are elected for six-year terms. There is currently no limit to the number of terms a senator can serve. Elections for one-third of the Senate seats are held once every two years. Potential senators must be at least 30 years old, a resident of the state they represent, and have been a U.S. citizen for at least nine years.

The House of Representatives   The number of congressional representatives varies with a state's population, as determined by the U.S. Census—currently 435 members serve in the House. Each state has at least one representative. The District of Columbia also has a single representative, although he or she does not vote. Most states are divided into districts and each member of the House represents his or her own district rather than the state as a whole. To qualify to be a representative, a person must be at least 25 years old, a resident of the state he or she represents, and have been a U.S. citizen for at least seven years. Duties of the House include introducing budget and tax bills to Congress and, in thankfully rare cases, impeaching government officials.

Shared Responsibilities   The Senate and House share these important duties: regulating money and printing currency; borrowing money on behalf of the government; levying and collecting taxes; regulating trade between states and with foreign countries; regulating the system of weights and measures; maintaining the defense and declaring war; maintaining the army, navy, and air force; making laws regarding naturalization; establishing post offices; and passing laws to govern the District of Columbia.

Legislative Branch Don'ts   The Constitution also lists some things that Congress may *never* do, specifically: tax exports, pass trade laws that do not treat all the states equally, spend tax money without a law that authorizes said spending, authorize any titles of nobility, pass any law that punishes someone for an act that was legal when the act was committed, or pass any law that takes away a person's right to trial in court.

THE JUDICIAL BRANCH

Made up of a system of hierarchical federal courts, the judicial branch is responsible for interpreting our laws. Federal court duties include explaining the meaning of the Constitution and the laws of the United States and its treaties, settling legal disagreements between citizens of different states, settling disputes between two or more states, settling legal questions between the states and the federal government, settling legal disputes between individuals and the federal government, settling disagreements between states and foreign governments or their citizens, and naturalizing United States citizens.

The Supreme Court   The highest court of the land as established by the Constitution, the Supreme Court makes rulings that constitute the final decision on a case. Presided over by nine judges or justices, the Supreme Court can overturn decisions made by lower courts as well as declare state or federal laws unconstitutional.

Circuit Court of Appeals   The country's 11 circuit courts routinely hear appeals from lower courts when their participants believe that justice was not properly served.

District Courts   The lowest of the federal courts, district courts determine rulings for people accused of breaking federal laws.

Special Courts   Congress has also established some special courts with very specific jurisdiction: Court of Claims, Customs Court, Court of Customs and Patent Appeals, and Court of Military Appeals.

Understand How and Why the Electoral College System Elects Our President

MANY PEOPLE ARE SURPRISED to learn the president and vice president of the United States are not directly elected by a popular vote, but rather are elected by members of the Electoral College—a group of elected officials from the 50 states and the District of Columbia.

In 1787, after rejecting many proposals relating to how we would elect our president, some of the framers of the Constitution believed the selection of the president should be left to the U.S.

Congress or to each state's legislature. These plans were ultimately rejected, as they skewed the balance of power between the federal and state governments. The Founding Fathers, not completely trusting the judgment of the people, also rejected the idea of their directly electing the commander in chief by a popular vote. Article II, Section 1 of the Constitution represents the final compromise—a system where each state is represented by the same number of electors as the state has U.S. senators and representatives. This gave each state representation based upon population. The distribution of electoral votes among the states can vary every 10 years, depending on the results of the census, so fill out those forms! While the Electoral College system remains controversial to this day, it would be necessary to pass a constitutional amendment to change it.

HOW CAN I BECOME AN ELECTOR?

The procedure for selecting electors varies state by state, but usually political parties nominate electors. Being selected as an elector is regarded as a prestigious honor, often given in recognition for service and dedication to the party. The voters of each state then finalize the choice on the day of the general election, although they may not know that's what they are actually doing. Depending on the individual state's election procedures, the electors' names may or may not appear on the ballot below the name of their corresponding candidate, but your vote for president is really a vote for the elector of that candidate's party. For information on the electoral process, you may wish to contact the Secretary of State's office in your state.

Not just anybody can be an elector. The U.S. Constitution contains a few rules on the matter. Article II, Section 1, Clause 2 provides that no senator or representative, or person holding an office of trust or profit under the United States, shall be appointed an elector. An interesting historical side note that relates to the post–Civil War era is found in the 14th amendment, which disqualifies state officials who have engaged in insurrection or rebellion against the United States, or given aid and comfort to its enemies, from becoming electors.

THE DOWNSIDE OF THE ELECTORAL COLLEGE

There is no Constitutional provision or federal law that requires electors to vote according to the results of the popular vote in their states, so it is possible for a candidate to win the popular vote but lose the electoral vote. To be sure, any candidate who wins a majority of the popular vote has a good chance of winning in the Electoral College, but there are no guarantees. To reduce the chances of this uncomfortable situation arising, some states require electors to pledge to cast their votes according to the popular vote. These pledges fall into two categories—electors bound by state law and those bound by pledges to political parties. Although the penalties and fines vary from nothing or replacement by another elector, to a fourth-degree felony in New Mexico, the following states all have some type of law governing electors: Alabama, Alaska, California, Colorado, Connecticut, District of Columbia, Florida, Hawaii, Maine, Maryland, Massachusetts, Michigan, Mississippi, Montana, Nebraska, Nevada, New Mexico, North Carolina, Ohio, Oklahoma, Oregon, South Carolina, Vermont, Virginia, Washington, Wisconsin, and Wyoming. Electors in the remaining states are expected to vote according to popular vote, but are not compelled to do so.

Forty-eight states have a winner-takes-all rule for the Electoral College, meaning whichever candidate receives a majority of the vote takes all of the state's electoral votes. In Nebraska and Maine, there could conceivably be a split of electoral votes.

The National Archives and Record Administration's Electoral College Homepage: *www.archives.gov/federal-register/electoral-college*

Understand Campaign Finance

THE FEDERAL ELECTION COMMISSION (FEC) serves as the independent regulatory government agency that administers and enforces the federal campaign finance law. The FEC has jurisdiction over the financing of campaigns for Congress, the presidency, and the vice presidency.

The Federal Election Campaign Act (FECA) requires candidates, candidate committees, party committees, and political action committees (PACs) to file periodic reports disclosing the money they raise and spend. Campaign laws are many and complex, but some highlights to keep in mind, should you be curious or want to make a political donation are:

- Candidates must identify all PACs and party committees that contribute to them as well as individuals who give them more than $200 in a year.

- Candidates must also disclose expenditures exceeding $200 per year to any individual or vendor.

- The following are prohibited from making contributions or expenditures to influence federal elections: labor organizations, federal government contractors, and foreign nationals.

- While corporations and labor organizations are not allowed to make contributions or expenditures in connection with federal elections, they may establish political action committees that support federal candidates and political committees. PACs raise voluntary contributions from a restricted class of individuals.

- No one may make a contribution in another person's name.

- No one may make a contribution in cash of more than $100.

- Foreign nationals, national banks, and other federally chartered corporations cannot make contributions or expenditures in connection with state and local elections.

- Most political state and national party committees as well as some local committees must file reports disclosing their federal campaign activities.

- Party committees may contribute funds directly to federal candidates, subject to contribution limits.

- State and local party committees may spend unlimited amounts on certain grassroots activities specified in the law without affecting their other contribution and expenditure limits.

☆ Hard vs. Soft Money

In any discussion of campaign finance, you'll hear the terms hard and soft money being batted around by the debaters. It's important to understand the difference. Hard money is given to specific candidates by individual donors. The amount an individual or corporation may donate is limited, adjusted for inflation each fiscal year. The FEC Web site will give you the latest amounts. Soft money donations are given to political parties, as opposed to specific candidates.

THE BIPARTISAN CAMPAIGN REFORM ACT OF 2002

Things on the campaign front changed after the November election of 2002, since President Bush signed H.R. 2356 into law in March 2002. The law alters the way politicians can raise money for election campaigns, banning unregulated donations of hundreds of thousands of dollars, known as "soft money," to political parties from individuals, corporations, and unions, while raising the limit on contributions from individual citizens.

Supporters believe the law curtails the ability of large corporations to buy political favor. Detractors say that limiting campaign funding, in effect, limits free speech. The debate is ongoing. Here are the principle points of H.R. 2356.

- Puts an end to national parties receiving unlimited soft money contributions. The new campaign law also stipulates that soft donations be used only for get-out-the-vote and voter registration efforts.

- Doubles the amount of regulated hard money an individual can contribute to a federal campaign, and indexes future increases for inflation. Currently an individual can donate $2,300.

- To help level the playing field, the law triples limits on hard money for congressional candidates who are running against wealthy opponents.

THE PRESIDENTIAL ELECTION FUND

We've all seen the question on our income tax returns that asks if we want to contribute to the Presidential Election Campaign Fund, but many people don't really understand what it means if they check "yes."

Checking the box will not affect the amount of taxes you pay, it simply allows the U.S. Treasury to direct $3 of your taxes (up to $6 for joint filers) to be used for presidential elections. Under the Internal Revenue Code, qualified presidential candidates receive money from the fund in the following three ways:

Primary Matching Payments   Eligible presidential primary candidates may receive public funds to match the private contributions they raise. Only contributions from individuals are matchable, and while an individual may give up to $2,000 to a primary candidate, the fund will only match up to $250 of that donation. In order to qualify for matching funds, a candidate must raise more than $5,000 in matchable contributions from donors in at least twenty different states. The Election Fund money can only be used for campaign expenses and the candidates must comply with spending limits.

General Election Grants   The Republican and Democratic candidates are each eligible to receive a grant to cover all the expenses of their general election campaigns. They, too, can only use the funds for campaign expenses and they must limit their campaign spending to the money they receive from public funds. In other words, they cannot accept contributions from individuals, PACs or party committees.

Party Convention Grants   The other major political parties may receive Election Fund money to pay for their national presidential nominating convention.

The Federal Election Commission Web site can give you all kinds of election data, rules, regulations, and information: *www.fec.gov*.

Learn About the CIA

CREATED IN 1947 WITH the signing of the National Security Act by President Truman, the Central Intelligence Agency (CIA) serves as an independent agency, responsible to the pesident through its director. In addition to providing our commander in chief with timely, accurate foreign intelligence, the CIA may, as directed by the president, conduct counterintelligence activities and other functions related to national security.

Even though the CIA was established as an independent agency, our government's system of checks and balances is still hard at work. Covert actions can only be initiated by the president, but once ordered, the Director of Central Intelligence must notify the intelligence oversight committees in the U.S. Congress. Congressional committees scrutinize the agency's activities, and the CIA must also adhere to specific laws that limit its activities. For instance, the CIA's specific duty is to collect information related to foreign intelligence and foreign counterintelligence. The law prohibits them from collecting foreign intelligence concerning the domestic activities of U.S. citizens and restricts collecting information directed against U.S. citizens in international matters. In rare instances, exceptions are made to this last rule—usually in cases of international terrorism or espionage activities. Even then, it's a complicated matter that requires senior CIA approval and often the sanctions of the Attorney

General of the United States and the Director of Central Intelligence.

If all this sounds like a spy movie, it is. The CIA even develops and uses cutting edge, high-tech means for gathering information and works closely with other organizations in the intelligence community to ensure they deliver the most accurate information in the most timely manner possible, to best equip our leaders to protect our national security.

TOURING THE CIA

As a matter of national security, public tours of Agency facilities are not permitted. You can, however, take a virtual tour of the CIA on their Web site at *www.cia.gov*.

WORLD FACTBOOK

One of the most useful benefits the public receives from the CIA's work is access to their *World Factbook*, which gives readers a snapshot profile of every country and territory in the world. *The World Factbook* covers history, geography, population, government, economy, transportation, community, and military statistics. Sometimes there's no better way to appreciate living in the United States than to learn about the rest of the world.

You can download the *Factbook* for free from the CIA Web site. You may also order a print copy from:

Superintendent of Documents
P. O. Box 371954
Pittsburgh, PA 15250-7954
Telephone: (202) 512-1800; or toll-free (866) 512-1800
http://bookstore.gpo.gov

THE INCEPTION OF THE National Aeronautics and Space Administration (NASA) in 1958 ushered in a new era of unique scientific and technological achievements in human space flight, aeronautics, space science, and space applications.

Formed as a result of the USSR getting the jump on the United States when it came to space exploration during the Cold War years, NASA took over where the National Advisory Committee for Aeronautics (NACA) left off. Beginning with Project *Mercury*, which determined whether or not humans could survive in space, through Project *Gemini*, which put two astronauts into space at the same time, and the *Apollo 11* mission that landed the first humans on the moon, NASA has led the way toward many great scientific and technological achievements.

Following the *Skylab* and *Apollo–Soyuz* test projects of the early and mid-1970s, human space flights took a hiatus until the launching of the space shuttle program that continues today. In addition, unmanned NASA scientific probes such as the *Pioneer* and *Voyager* spacecraft have explored the Moon, the planets, and other areas of our solar system. The Hubble Space Telescope and other unmanned spacecraft have led scientists to a number of significant astronomical discoveries about the universe we call home.

Five Strategic Enterprises comprise NASA's overall program. Here's the breakdown, according to NASA sources:

Aerospace Technology   Pioneers the identification, development, verification, transfer, application, and commercialization of high-payoff aeronautics and space transportation technologies.

Biological and Physical Research   Conducts basic and applied research to support human exploration of space and to take advantage of the space environment as a laboratory for scientific, technological, and commercial research. This department asks questions basic to our future: How can human existence expand beyond the home planet to achieve maximum benefits from space? How do fundamental laws of nature shape the evolution of life?

Earth Science   Uses the unique vantage point of space to provide information about Earth's environment that is obtainable in no other way. In concert with research and industry partners, the Earth Science Enterprise is developing the understanding needed to support the complex environmental policy and economic investment decisions that lie ahead.

Human Exploration and Development of Space   Seeks to open the space frontier by exploring, using, and enabling the development of space and to expand the human experience into the far reaches of space. This enterprise provides transportation to and from space for people and payloads, and develops and operates habitable space facilities that enhance scientific knowledge, support technology development, and enable commercial activity.

Space Science   Seeks to solve mysteries of the universe, explore the solar system, discover planets around other stars, search for life beyond Earth from origins to destiny, chart the evolution of the universe, and understand its galaxies, stars, planets, and life.

VIEWING A LAUNCH

NASA and the Department of Defense operate several launch facilities. If you plan to view a space launch, keep in mind that schedules change frequently and often at the last minute, so always call or check Web sites for the latest details. Here are the main NASA launch facilities:

Kennedy Space Center   Due to security precautions since the events of September 11, 2001, NASA has suspended issuing car passes for launch viewing from inside of the Kennedy Space Center. However, a limited number of launch transportation tickets for viewing space shuttle and expendable launch vehicle launches may be available through the Kennedy Space Center Visitor Complex. Luckily, you can also find lots of prime viewing areas outside of the space center along U.S. highway 1 in the city of Titusville and along highway A1A in the cities of Cape Canaveral and Cocoa Beach on the Atlantic Ocean. The Kennedy Space Center Web site gives details about offsite launch viewing. Adjacent to the Kennedy Center is Patrick Air Force Base, the Department of Defense launching facility. While there are no public viewing areas on the base, many of the launches can be seen from the beaches south of there.

Kennedy Space Center Contact Information

- The Center is located in Florida on S.R. 405 (aka the NASA Causeway) between the Kennedy Space Center (KSC) Industrial Area on Merritt Island to the east and U.S. 1 on the mainland to the west.

- For general information call the Kennedy Space Center Visitor Complex at (321) 452-2121 or TDD for the hearing impaired at (321) 454-4198.

- For anticipated launch dates call (321) 867-4636 or go to *www.nasa.gov/centers/kennedy/launchingrockets/viewing.html*.

- Visit the Kennedy Space Center Web site at *www.nasa.gov/centers/kennedy/home/index.html*.

Wallops Island   Wallops Island, Virginia, hosts NASA's launch facility for research aircraft, balloons, and sounding rockets. The best views can be seen from the NASA Visitor Center, located on Route 175 directly across from the Wallops runways and adjacent to the marsh. Televisions inside the Center give visitors a behind-the-scenes look at activities on the launch pad. In addition to the Wallops Web page, which lists both monthly and daily launch schedules, the public can get the latest information by calling the Wallops Public Information Line at (757) 824-2050. If you can't make it to Wallops in person, you can view launches live via the Internet. Coverage begins approximately 30 minutes before the scheduled launch: *www.nasa.gov/centers/wallops/home/index.html*.

VISITING NASA

The general public is welcome to visit and tour many NASA installations. Some NASA Centers operate their own visitors' centers, others have contractual arrangements with private firms. Admission fees are charged at some sites. To check on hours, fees, and tour availability, visit *www.nasa.gov/about/visiting*.

ADDITIONAL INFORMATION

The National Aeronautics and Space Administration covers a lot of territory, and their Web site at *www.nasa.gov* is the best place to learn about all their latest activities and accomplishments. In addition to the programs outlined above, you'll find tons of fascinating articles about everything from the effect of gravity on the human brain to microscopic stowaways on the international space station.

HOUSING A COLLECTION OF more than 134 million items in 460 languages, including the largest map, film, and television collections in the world, and employing a staff of more than 4,000 people, the Library of Congress is the globe's largest library.

Thanks to an aggressive acquisitions program that extends throughout the world and includes over 15,000 agreements with foreign governments and research institutions, the rate at which the library collections expand staggers the imagination. Each day about 22,000 items arrive, approximately 10,000 of which will become part of the permanent collections.

Founded upon the vision of Founding Father Thomas Jefferson, whose own personal library provided the basis for what was to grow into the Library of Congress, the library's primary goal is to serve as a legislative library and research arm of the U.S. Congress. Jefferson believed there was no subject on earth that Congress might not need information about at one time or another, hence the massive scope of the library's collections.

Thomas Jefferson also believed that it takes an involved citizenry to make democracy work, and as such, all Americans over high school age are welcome to access the library through its 22 reading rooms on Capitol Hill. Millions more access the online Virtual Library of Congress each year at *www.loc.gov*.

VISITING THE LIBRARY

The Library of Congress occupies three massive structures on Capitol Hill, near the U.S. Capitol building. About 1 million researchers, scholars, and tourists visit the Library of Congress annually. Docent-led tours, beginning in the Ground Floor Visitors Center of the Thomas Jefferson Building, are offered at 10:30 and 11:30 a.m. and 1:30, 2:30, and 3:30 p.m., Monday through Saturday (although there is no 3:30 tour on Saturdays). For more information, call the Visitor Services Office at (202) 707-9779 or e-mail *vso@loc.gov*. Don't forget, your elected officials can also arrange special library tours. See the chapter about visiting Washington, DC, for more information.

Library of Congress Information Numbers and Mailing Address

- General Information: (202) 707-5000

- Reading Room Hours: (202) 707-6400

- Researchers' Information: (202) 707-6500

- Visitors' Information: (202) 707-8000

- Directions to the Library: (202) 707-4700

- Chamber Music Concerts: (202) 707-5502

- Pickford Theater Showings: (202) 707-5677

- The Library of Congress
    101 Independence Avenue SE
    Washington, DC 20540

While the Library of Congress may be the world's largest, the libraries in your hometown still have a lot to offer. To find out what facilities are close to you, the National Center for Education Statistics Web site lets you locate libraries in communities across the country: *www.nces.ed.gov.*

Learn About Social Security

ONE OF THE LARGEST domestic government programs, Social Security was designed to provide you and your family with economic disability, survivor, and retirement protection. Contrary to what many people believe, the government never intended for Social Security benefits to be your only source of income when you retire or become disabled, or your family's only revenue if you die. Social Security is meant to supplement other income you have from pension plans, savings, and investments.

Throughout your life, as you work and pay taxes, you earn "credits" that count toward eligibility for future Social Security payment benefits. According to the Social Security Administration (SSA), low income workers receive an overall higher rate of return than those in the upper income brackets, but a worker with average earnings can expect a retirement benefit that represents about 40 percent of his or her average lifetime earnings. You can get a free estimate of the retirement, disability, and survivors benefits that would be payable to you and your family by calling the SSA toll-free at

1-800-772-1213, or you can calculate your own benefits online using the handy tool at the SSA's Web site: *www.ssa.gov*.

According to the SSA, you can qualify to receive Social Security benefits in six ways:

Retirement   If you were born before 1938, full retirement age, as determined by the SSA, is age 65. This was gradually adjusted upward to age 67 for persons born in 1960 or later. Full Social Security benefits become payable when you reach full retirement age, although you're welcome to retire with reduced benefits as early as age 62. On the other hand, those who delay retirement beyond SSA full retirement age get a special credit incentive for each month they don't receive benefits until they reach age 70.

Disability   People of any age who have severe physical or mental impairments that prevent them from performing "substantial" work for a year or more, or who have a condition that is expected to result in death, are eligible to collect Social Security benefits at any age, provided they've earned enough Social Security credits earlier in life. The disability program also includes incentives to smooth the transition back into the workforce, including continuation of benefits and health care coverage while a person attempts to work.

Family Benefits   If you are eligible for retirement or disability benefits, other members of your family might also be eligible to receive benefits: your spouse, if he or she is at least 62 years old (or under 62 but caring for a child under age 16), and your children, if they are unmarried and under age 18 (or under 19 but still in school, or 18 or older but disabled). If you are divorced, your ex-spouse might also be eligible for benefits on your record.

Survivors   If you earned enough Social Security credits while you were working, certain family members may be eligible for Social Security benefits if you die, including a widow(er) age 60 or older, 50 or older if disabled, or any age if caring for a child under age 16; your children if they are unmarried and under age 18, under 19 but still in school, or 18 or older but disabled; and your parents if you were their primary means of support. A special onetime payment of $255 may also be made to your spouse or minor children in the event of your death. If you are divorced, your ex-spouse could also be eligible for a widow(er)'s benefit on your record.

Medicare   There are two parts to Medicare: hospital insurance (Part A), which helps pay for inpatient hospital care, skilled nursing care, and other services; and medical insurance (Part B), which helps pay for doctors' fees, outpatient hospital visits, and other medical services and supplies. Generally, people who are over age 65 and getting Social Security, as well as those who have been receiving disability benefits for at least two years, automatically qualify for Medicare. Others must file an application.

Supplemental Security Income   SSI makes monthly payments to people who have a low income and few assets. To get SSI, you must be 65 or older or be disabled. As its name implies, Supplemental Security Income "supplements" income up to various levels—depending on where the recipient lives. The federal government pays a basic rate which some states supplement with additional money. Check with your local Social Security office for the SSI rates in your state. Usually, people who get SSI also qualify for Medicaid, food stamps, and other assistance. Supplemental Security Income benefits are not paid from Social Security trust funds nor are they based on your past earnings.

YOUR SOCIAL SECURITY NUMBER

Your Social Security number serves as a way for the Social Security Administration to keep track of your earnings and the number of Social Security credits you've earned over the course of your life. As the number of credits determines the amount of benefits you'll receive, it's important to always use your proper Social Security number and make sure the name you give your employer matches the one on your Social Security card. The SSA does not charge to update your Social Security card should your name ever change, but failing to do so could result in lack of benefits for you later on.

Today, everyone needs a Social Security number, even infants if their parents want to claim them as dependents for tax purposes.

SOCIAL SECURITY FACTS AND TRIVIA

- President Franklin Delano Roosevelt signed the Social Security Act on August 14, 1935.

- The first Social Security taxes were collected and the first benefits paid out in January of 1937.

- Until January 1940, when the Social Security Administration started ongoing monthly payments, Social Security benefits were paid out in one single lump sum.

- Social Security numbers were first issued in November 1936.

- Cleveland, Ohio, motorman Ernest Ackerman, who retired one day after the Social Security Administration began, became the first Social Security recipient when he received a onetime lump sum payment of 17 cents in January 1937.

- On January 31, 1940, Ida May Fuller of Ludlow, Vermont, collected the first monthly Social Security benefit check in the amount of $22.54. A former legal secretary, Ida May started collecting retirement benefits in 1940 at age 65 and continued to receive benefits until she passed away at age 100.

- Social Security payroll taxes are collected under authority of the Federal Insurance Contributions Act (FICA). Payroll taxes are sometimes even called "FICA taxes."

- Over 420 million different Social Security numbers have been issued to date.

- The first three digits tell where you lived when you first got a Social Security number. Generally, numbers were assigned beginning in the northeast and moving westward, so people born on the East Coast have the low numbers and those on the West Coast have the high numbers.

- The remaining six digits of your Social Security number are assigned more or less randomly, according to the needs of the Social Security Administration of the 1930s, which kept records by hand.

- When a person dies, his or her Social Security number dies with them. The SSA simply removes the number from the active files. While they do have the authority to recycle numbers, it would be a long time before the need to recycle would arise, as our nine-digit Social Security numbers provide about a billion possible combinations.

- From 1937 (when the first payments were made) through 2005, the Social Security program paid out more than $8.9 trillion in cash benefits, and has taken in $10.7 trillion from taxes and other revenues.

- To date, there have been 11 years when the Social Security program did not take enough in FICA taxes to pay the current year's benefits. Trust Fund bonds in the amount of about $24 billion made up the difference.

ADDITIONAL INFORMATION

Since Social Security is only meant to supplement your retirement income, it's vital to plan ahead. The Federal Consumer Information Center offers many free publications to help you budget, save money, and invest and prepare for your retirement. For information on how to order print copies, see the chapter on how to be an informed consumer. You can also access the information online by entering the word "retirement" in the search box at *www.pueblo.gsa.gov*.

HERE IS A LISTING of the all presidents of the United States in order of their terms in office. Memorize this list and you'll always be prepared should you ever get on a TV quiz show!

1. George Washington, 1789–1797
2. John Adams, 1797–1801
3. Thomas Jefferson, 1801–1809
4. James Madison, 1809–1817
5. James Monroe, 1817–1825
6. John Quincy Adams, 1825–1829
7. Andrew Jackson, 1829–1837
8. Martin Van Buren, 1837–1841
9. William Henry Harrison, 1841
10. John Tyler, 1841–1845
11. James Knox Polk, 1845–1849
12. Zachary Taylor, 1849–1850
13. Millard Fillmore, 1850–1853
14. Franklin Pierce, 1853–1857
15. James Buchanan, 1857–1861
16. Abraham Lincoln, 1861–1865
17. Andrew Johnson, 1865–1869
18. Ulysses Simpson Grant, 1869–1877
19. Rutherford Birchard Hayes, 1877–1881
20. James Abram Garfield, 1881
21. Chester Alan Arthur, 1881–1885
22. Grover Cleveland, 1885–1889
23. Benjamin Harrison, 1889–1893
24. Grover Cleveland, 1893–1897
25. William McKinley, 1897–1901
26. Theodore Roosevelt, 1901–1909
27. William Howard Taft, 1909–1913
28. Woodrow Wilson, 1913–1921
29. Warren Gamaliel Harding, 1921–1923
30. Calvin Coolidge, 1923–1929
31. Herbert Clark Hoover, 1929–1933
32. Franklin Delano Roosevelt, 1933–1945
33. Harry S. Truman, 1945–1953
34. Dwight David Eisenhower 1953–1961
35. John Fitzgerald Kennedy, 1961–1963
36. Lyndon Baines Johnson, 1963–1969
37. Richard Milhous Nixon, 1969–1974
38. Gerald Rudolph Ford, 1974–1977
39. James Earl Carter, Jr., 1977–1981
40. Ronald Wilson Reagan, 1981–1989
41. George Herbert Walker Bush, 1989–1993
42. William Jefferson Clinton, 1993–2001
43. George Walker Bush, 2001–2008

ADDITIONAL INFORMATION

- The White House Web site offers biographies of all our presidents: *www.whitehouse.gov/history/presidents*.

- Inaugural addresses of the presidents can be read at: *www.bartleby.com/124*.

State/Postal Abbreviation	Capital	Date of Statehood	Population as of 2000 Census	Nickname
Alabama (AL)	Montgomery	December 14, 1819	4,447,100	Heart of Dixie, Yellowhammer State, Cotton State
Alaska (AK)	Juneau	January 3, 1959	626,932	The Last Frontier
Arizona (AZ)	Phoenix	February 14, 1912	5,130,632	Grand Canyon State
Arkansas (AR)	Little Rock	June 15, 1836	2,673,400	The Natural State, Land of Opportunity
California (CA)	Sacramento	September 9, 1850	33,871,648	Golden State
Colorado (CO)	Denver	August 1, 1876	4,301,261	Centennial State
Connecticut (CT)	Hartford	January 9, 1788	3,405,565	Constitution State, Nutmeg State
Delaware (DE)	Dover	December 7, 1787	783,600	First State, Diamond State, Blue Hen State
Florida (FL)	Tallahassee	March 3, 1845	15,982,378	Sunshine State
Georgia (GA)	Atlanta	January 2, 1788	8,186,453	Peach State, Goober State
Hawaii (HI)	Honolulu	August 21, 1959	1,211,537	Aloha State, Pineapple State
Idaho (ID)	Boise	July 3, 1890	1,293,953	Gem State
Illinois (IL)	Springfield	December 3, 1818	12,419,293	Land of Lincoln, Prairie State
Indiana (IN)	Indianapolis	December 11, 1816	6,080,485	Hoosier State
Iowa (IA)	Des Moines	December 28, 1846	2,926,324	Hawkeye State
Kansas (KS)	Topeka	January 29, 1861	2,688,418	Sunflower State
Kentucky (KY)	Frankfort	June 1, 1792	4,041,769	Bluegrass State
Louisiana (LA)	Baton Rouge	April 30, 1812	4,468,976	Pelican State
Maine (ME)	Augusta	March 15, 1820	1,274,923	Pine Tree State
Maryland (MD)	Annapolis	April 28, 1788	5,296,486	Old Line State, Free State
Massachusetts (MA)	Boston	February 6, 1788	6,349,097	Bay State
Michigan (MI)	Lansing	January 26, 1837	9,938,444	Great Lakes State, Wolverine State

State	Capital	Statehood	Population	Nickname
Minnesota (MN)	St. Paul	May 11, 1858	4,919,479	North Star State, Gopher State, Land of 10,000 Lakes
Mississippi (MS)	Jackson	December 10, 1817	2,844,658	Magnolia State
Missouri (MO)	Jefferson City	August 10, 1821	5,595,211	Show Me State
Montana (MT)	Helena	November 8, 1889	902,195	Treasure State, Big Sky State
Nebraska (NE)	Lincoln	March 1, 1867	1,711,263	Cornhusker State
Nevada (NV)	Carson City	October 31, 1864	1,998,257	Silver State
New Hampshire (NH)	Concord	June 21, 1788	1,235,786	Granite State
New Jersey (NJ)	Trenton	December 18, 1787	8,414,350	Garden State
New Mexico (NM)	Santa Fe	January 6, 1912	1,819,046	Land of Enchantment
New York (NY)	Albany	July 26, 1788	18,976,457	Empire State
North Carolina (NC)	Raleigh	November 21, 1789	8,049,313	Tar Heel State, Old North State
North Dakota (ND)	Bismarck	November 2, 1889	642,200	Peace Garden State, Roughrider State
Ohio (OH)	Columbus	March 1, 1803	11,353,140	Buckeye State
Oklahoma (OK)	Oklahoma City	November 16, 1907	3,450,654	Sooner State
Oregon (OR)	Salem	February 14, 1859	3,421,399	Beaver State
Pennsylvania (PA)	Harrisburg	December 12, 1787	12,281,054	Keystone State, Quaker State
Rhode Island (RI)	Providence	May 29, 1790	1,048,319	Ocean State, Little Rhody
South Carolina (SC)	Columbia	May 23, 1788	4,012,012	Palmetto State
South Dakota (SD)	Pierre	November 2, 1889	754,844	Mount Rushmore State
Tennessee (TN)	Nashville	June 1, 1796	5,689,283	Volunteer State
Texas (TX)	Austin	December 29, 1845	20,851,820	Lone Star State
Utah (UT)	Salt Lake City	January 4, 1896	2,233,169	Beehive State
Vermont (VT)	Montpelier	March 4, 1791	608,827	Green Mountain State
Virginia (VA)	Richmond	June 25, 1788	7,078,515	Old Dominion
Washington (WA)	Olympia	November 11, 1889	5,894,121	Evergreen State
West Virginia (WV)	Charleston	June 20, 1863	1,808,344	Mountain State
Wisconsin (WI)	Madison	May 29, 1848	5,363,675	Badger State
Wyoming (WY)	Cheyenne	July 10, 1890	493,782	Equality State, Cowboy State

- **American Samoa** International rivalries in the late 19th century resulted in an 1899 treaty in which Germany and the United States divided the Samoan archipelago, with the United States occupying a small group of eastern islands.

- **Baker Island** Early attempts to colonize the island failed. Baker Island is now a national wildlife refuge run by the U.S. Department of the Interior.

- **Commonwealth of Northern Mariana** Formerly under U.S. administration as part of the U.N. Trust Territory of the Pacific, a covenant to establish a commonwealth in political union with the United States was approved in 1975 and the islands' new government and constitution took effect in 1978.

- **Guam** Ceded to the United States by Spain in 1898, then captured by the Japanese in 1941, the United States regained control of the island three years later. Guam's military installation remains one of the most strategically important U.S. bases in the entire Pacific.

- **Howland Island** Officially claimed by the U.S. in 1857, both U.S. and British companies mined for guano here until about 1890. The island is currently administered by the U.S. Department of the Interior as a national wildlife refuge.

- **Jarvis Island** Annexed by the United States in 1858, but abandoned in 1879 after tons of guano had been mined, Jarvis Island was annexed by the United Kingdom in 1889, then reclaimed by the United States in 1935. Abandoned after World War II, the island is currently a national wildlife refuge.

- **Johnston Atoll**   Annexed in 1858 by both the United States and the Kingdom of Hawaii, the U.S. Navy took over the atoll in 1934, then relinquished control to the U.S. Air Force in 1948. The site was used for high altitude nuclear tests in the 1950s and 1960s, and served as a storage and disposal site for chemical weapons until late 2000. Cleanup and closure of the facility is currently in progress.

- **Kingman Reef**   The United States annexed the reef in 1922, using its sheltered lagoon as a way station on Hawaii–American Samoa flights during the late 1930s. In 2001, the waters surrounding the reef were designated a national wildlife refuge.

- **Midway Islands**   The United States took formal possession of the Midway Islands in 1867. The site of the Battle of Midway—a pivotal turning point of World War II—the islands served as a refueling stop for trans-Pacific flights between 1935 and 1947. A navy base continued to operate here until 1993 when the Midway Islands became a wildlife refuge open to the public.

- **Navassa Island**   Claimed by the United States in 1857 and mined for its guano, this uninhabited island has otherwise been little more than a place to put a lighthouse. That beacon was permanently extinguished in 1996 when the administration of Navassa Island transferred from the Coast Guard to the Department of the Interior, who now maintain it as a national wildlife refuge.

- **Palmyra Atoll**   The Kingdom of Hawaii originally laid claim to Palmyra Atoll in 1862. Although the United States counted it among the Hawaiian Islands when they were annexed in

1898, the Hawaii Statehood Act of 1959 did not include it. The island is now privately owned by the Nature Conservancy, who manage it as a nature reserve. The U.S. Fish and Wildlife service administers the atoll's lagoons and surrounding waters, now designated as a national wildlife refuge.

- **Puerto Rico**   Columbus claimed Puerto Rico for the Spanish in 1493. The United States gained control of the island in 1898 following the Spanish-American War. Why doesn't Puerto Rico become a state? In public elections held in 1967 and 1993, voters chose to keep their commonwealth status.

- **Virgin Islands**   During the 17th century, the islands were split into two territorial units, one English and the other Danish. The United States purchased the Danish portion in 1917, after the banning of slavery left the Virgin Islands in economic decline.

- **Wake Island**   Originally annexed in 1899 for use as a cable station, the island was later groomed to serve as an important air and naval base during World War II. Unfortunately, the Japanese captured it in 1941. In the years since, Wake Island's airstrip has been in continual use as a refueling and emergency landing stop for U.S. military as well as commercial cargo planes.

According to the CIA's *World Factbook*, from July 18, 1947, until October 1, 1994, the United States administered the Trust Territory of the Pacific Islands, but recently entered into a new political relationship with these four political units:

- **The Northern Mariana Islands** became a commonwealth in political union with the United States.

- **Palau,** the **Federated States of Micronesia** and the **Republic of the Marshall Islands** signed a Compact of Free Association with the United States.

Learn About Our National Motto— In God We Trust

INCREASED RELIGIOUS SENTIMENT DURING the Civil War is largely responsible for the motto "In God We Trust" appearing on United States currency. Despite being barraged with appeals urging the United States to recognize God on coins, then Secretary of the Treasury Salmon P. Chase had his hands tied since an 1837 Act of Congress specifically prescribed exactly which mottoes and devices could be placed on U.S. currency. It took another Act of Congress to change that and it occurred on April 22, 1864. The words "In God We Trust" were first seen that year on the newly minted two-cent coins. More congressional acts throughout the years have authorized the motto to appear on various other currency denominations.

Although all U.S. coins have borne the inscription since 1938, the use of the motto has not been uninterrupted. According to the Treasury Department, the words disappeared from the five-cent coin in 1883, and did not reappear until production of the Jefferson nickel in 1938. The motto has been in continuous use on the penny since 1909, on the dime since 1916, and on all gold coins, silver dollars, half-dollars, and quarter coins struck since July 1, 1908. But it took until July 11, 1955, for it to be officially written into law that the motto should appear on all U.S. paper currency and coins. This was one year before the words "In God We Trust" were officially adopted as the national motto of the United States of America on July 30, 1956.

The national motto comes with a certain degree of controversy, as the constitutionality of the words has been challenged on many occasions. Nevertheless, the courts, which tend to favor looking at the motto in a historical context, have consistently upheld the constitutionality of the motto's use on the basis that it is not an endorsement of religion.

Many people think the Latin words *E pluribus unum* (out of many, one) is the national motto. In fact, you can even find the words labeled as such in some government publications. While the Latin phrase is used in many patriotic emblems—including the Great Seal of the United States—"In God We Trust" remains the officially recognized national motto.

Know the American's Creed

MANY AMERICANS DON'T EVEN know we have a creed, much less what it is or how it came to be.

THE AMERICAN'S CREED

I believe in the United States of America as a government of the people, by the people, for the people; whose just powers are derived from the consent of the governed; a democracy in a republic, a sovereign nation of many sovereign states; a perfect union, one and inseparable, established upon those principles of freedom, equality, justice, and humanity for which American patriots sacrificed their lives and fortunes.

I therefore believe it is my duty to my country to love it, to support its Constitution, to obey its laws, to respect its flag, and to defend it against all enemies.

THE BACKGROUND BEHIND THE CREED

America's involvement in World War I was a difficult and divisive issue for our nation. President Woodrow Wilson struggled to maintain a position of American neutrality toward the European conflict. But when a German U-boat sank the unarmed British liner *Lusitania*, killing more than 1,000 people including 128 Americans on May 7, 1915, the president felt compelled to go before Congress to request a Declaration of War. Six U.S. senators and 50 representatives voted against the declaration, although after much heated debate, the resolution finally passed on April 6, 1917. Citizens protested America's involvement and thousands went to jail for interfering with the draft—protesting the war was in vogue long before Vietnam or Iraq.

It was in the midst of this domestic turmoil that New York State Commissioner of Education Henry Sterling Chapin hatched the idea of a national essay contest to develop an American's Creed. By the contest deadline, more than 3,000 entries were received. William Tyler Page of Friendship Heights, Maryland, a descendent of President John Tyler, and himself a congressional page, came up with the winning words. Tyler incorporated portions of the Declaration of Independence, the Preamble to the Constitution, and Lincoln's Gettysburg Address to echo the same strength and unity of American spirit that is still evident today. In America, some things remain constant. Originally penned in 1917, the Creed was officially accepted by the United States House of Representatives on April 3, 1918.

THE BALD EAGLE *(HALIAEETUS LEUCOCEPHALUS)*, our national bird, is the only eagle unique to North America. When America adopted the bird as its national symbol in 1782, as many as 100,000 nesting bald eagles lived in the continental United States, excluding Alaska, and the bald eagle populated every state in the union except Hawaii. By 1963, only 487 breeding pairs were counted in the lower 48 states. Eagle populations in Alaska and Canada have always been healthy.

Today, due to efforts by the Interior Department's U.S. Fish and Wildlife Service—in partnership with other federal agencies, tribes, state and local governments, conservation organizations, universities, corporations, and thousands of individual Americans—the number of breeding pairs in the lower 48 states has risen to an estimated 9,789.

Congress passed the Bald Eagle Protection Act in 1940, which prohibited the killing or selling of bald eagles. The Act increased public awareness of the bird, and populations stabilized or increased in most areas of the country. Shortly after World War II, however, the use of DDT and other organochlorine pesticides became widespread. Sprayed extensively along coastal and other wetland areas to control mosquitoes, eagles ingested the DDT by eating contaminated fish. The pesticide caused the shells of the bird's eggs to thin, resulting in large numbers of nesting failures. Loss of suitable nesting habitat lands also contributed to the eagle population decline.

In 1967, the Secretary of the Interior listed bald eagles south of the 40th parallel as "endangered," under the Endangered Species Preservation Act. In 1972, the Environmental Protection Agency took the historic—and, at the time, controversial— measure of banning the use of DDT in the United States. These first steps put the

American bald eagle population on the road to recovery.

In 1999, on the eve of Independence Day weekend, President Clinton marked the culmination of the three-decade effort to protect and recover our majestic national bird by announcing a proposal to remove it from the list of threatened and endangered species:

The American bald eagle is now back from the brink of extinction, thriving in virtually every state of the union. I can think of no better way to honor the birth of our nation than by celebrating the rebirth of our proudest living symbol.

★ Ben Franklin's Nomination for National Bird

Benjamin Franklin, one of our most respected Founding Fathers, disapproved of the choice of the bald eagle as the national bird. He believed the eagle was a bird of bad moral character as it steals food from other, weaker animals. Franklin thought the best bird for the job was none other than the humble turkey, which Franklin described as "a bird of courage that would not hesitate to attack a grenadier of the British guards, who should presume to invade his farmyard with a red coat on."

HOW TO SPOT A BALD EAGLE

Since the eagle was named the national bird, its image has regularly appeared on currency, official seals, and other patriotic illustrations. But did you know that many of these classic illustrations depict the golden, rather than the bald eagle?

So how can you tell if you're looking at the real thing? The easiest way to tell the two apart is by the feathering on the legs. The golden eagle sports feathers down his entire leg, while the bald eagle has no feathers on the lower part of his leg until he's at least two or three years of age, which is when he'll also start developing a white head and tail.

WHERE DO DEAD EAGLES GO?

Possessing an eagle or eagle parts, nests, or eggs in the United States carries a felony charge, but exceptions are made for federally recognized Native Americans who use the eagle as part of their religious ceremonies. By providing feathers to Native Americans, the government relieves the pressure to take birds from the wild, and thereby protects eagle populations.

U.S. law prohibits the selling, purchasing, bartering, or trading of feathers or parts of bald or golden eagles and other migratory birds, even by Native Americans. The artifacts may, however, be handed down to family members, from generation to generation, or from one Native American to another for religious purposes. Native Americans may not give eagle feathers or parts to anyone who is not a Native American.

So where does a modern day Native American get his ceremonial eagle or eagle parts? The National Eagle Repository at the Rocky Mountain Arsenal National Wildlife Refuge in Denver, Colorado. The repository serves as a collection point for dead eagles and provides a legal means for Native Americans to acquire eagle feathers for religious purposes.

State and federal wildlife personnel salvaged most of the birds in the repository. Each dead bird is assigned a number for tracking and accountability purposes, and a database records information about each eagle, noting the condition of the bird and its feathers, as well as species and estimated age. If part of a bird is missing, damaged, lacking feathers, or broken, repository staff may add replacement "parts" from another bird to make one complete eagle. Recipients will always be told of the replacement.

Requests for eagles are filled on a first-come, first-served basis. The birds are typically kept at the repository just long enough to allow for processing and to contact the next applicant on the waiting list—usually between three and five days. Due to high demand and short supply, applicants can expect to wait about two and a half years for their eagle order to be filled.

ADDITIONAL INFORMATION

Everything you ever wanted to know about bald eagles and then some, including state-by-state tips for viewing bald eagles, is at *www.baldeagleinfo.com*.

Learn About the Great Seal of the United States

OUR FOUNDING FATHERS BELIEVED an emblem and national coat of arms would help solidify the identity of the United States as an independent nation of free people. Benjamin Franklin, John Adams, and Thomas Jefferson undertook the task of creating the seal for the United States of America in 1776. Six years later on June 20, 1782, the Great Seal was finalized and approved.

The Secretary of State serves as the official custodian of the Great Seal and it can only be affixed to certain documents, such as foreign treaties and presidential proclamations. An officer from the State Department's presidential appointments staff does the actual embossing of documents after the Secretary of State has counter-signed the president's signature.

The Great Seal of the United States is rich with patriotic symbolism. Next time you gaze at, keep these points in mind:

- Central to the seal is a bald eagle, our national bird, holding in its beak a scroll inscribed *E pluribus unum*—Latin for "out of many, one," symbolizing how our 13 original colonies came together to form one nation.

- The eagle's right claw clutches an olive branch while the left talon holds 13 arrows, denoting "the power of peace and war."

- A shield with 13 red and white stripes covers the eagle's breast. Supported solely by the eagle, the shield reminds Americans to rely on their own virtue.

- The blue field on the shield represents the president and Congress, being supported by the states, denoted by the red and white stripes.

- As with our flag, red signifies hardiness and valor, white purity and innocence, and blue vigilance, perseverance, and justice.

- Floating above the eagle's head in a field of blue is a constellation formed of 13 stars. The constellation symbolized that America, a new state, was taking its place among other nations.

LUCKY THIRTEEN

A definite pattern of 13 repeats itself in many of the Great Seal's components. In addition to the more obvious examples stated above, even the motto, *E pluribus unum,* has 13 letters in it. The number represents the 13 original American colonies: Massachusetts, Connecticut, Rhode Island, New Hampshire, New York, New Jersey, Pennsylvania, Delaware, Virginia, Maryland, North Carolina, South Carolina, and Georgia.

THE BACK SIDE

- On the seal's reverse side you'll find a familiar image as it's also used on the back of U.S. dollar bills:

- An unfinished 13-step pyramid symbolizes strength and duration, and once again, the thirteen original colonies.

- Atop the pyramid is the Eye of Providence. The words *Annuit Coepti*s appear above the pyramid, meaning, "God has favored our undertakings."

- A scroll beneath the pyramid proclaims 1776 as the beginning of the American new era with the Latin words *Novus Ordo Seclorum*, meaning "New Order of the Ages."

SEE THE SEAL

The Great Seal, used to emboss the designs upon international treaties and other official U.S. government documents, is displayed in the Exhibit Hall of the Department of State, in Washington, DC.

Get News from a Variety of Sources

AMERICANS LARGELY RELY ON broadcast television for their news, although they also form opinions based on what they hear on the radio and to a lesser extent, read in newspapers, in magazines, and on the Internet. The wise American, however, gets information from all these sources, as it's impossible to cast informed votes or make knowledgeable decisions about public policy if the news on which you base those decisions is distorted.

Accusations of media bias fly from both the right and left political wings—and depending on the news report you're hearing, both sides are right. In fact, there are many reasons the news reporting of today differs from that of your grandfather's era. For one thing, large, for-profit corporations own almost all media that reach a large portion of the population. The goal of maximizing profits can sometimes be in conflict with responsible, unbiased journalism. As media giants become larger and fewer in number, with the biggest ones absorbing their smaller rivals, Americans are faced with a reduced diversity of media voices to choose from. For instance, many radio stations, television stations, and newspapers all get their stories and articles from the exact same syndicate source.

Large media corporations also often own significant holdings in other industries. A good thing for the media consumer to keep in mind is, the larger the parent corporation, the greater the chance for internal conflicts of interest.

For-profit news organizations are under tremendous pressure to boost ratings or increase sales, which often results in the sensationalizing of the news. From Paris Hilton and Britney Spears to O. J. Simpson, Phil Spector, Jon Benet Ramsey, and Anna Nicole Smith, the media will always focus an undue amount of attention on sensational, highly emotional stories—even if those stories have no major significance to the public's lives. Such lurid tales used to be relegated to the tabloid press, but the enticements of higher ratings have caused them to creep into our nightly news.

So what can the average citizen do to stay informed? Follow these tips, then form you own opinions based upon all the facts:

- Get your news from as wide a variety of media as possible—watch television, listen to the radio, and read different newspapers or Internet accounts of the same story.

- Various newspapers are generally known to lean toward the right or the left; try to read at least one of each to get both sides of the story.

- Try to get news and views from nonprofit as well as for-profit sources (nonprofit sources include National Public Radio, the Public Broadcasting System, and the publications of various nonprofit organizations).

ADDITIONAL INFORMATION: BECOME A MEDIA ACTIVIST

Take a stand and fight media bias by becoming actively involved. Fairness and Accuracy in Reporting (FAIR), a national media watchgroup, can get you started. FAIR has been offering well-documented criticism of media bias and censorship since 1986. The organization advocates greater diversity in the press, works to expose important news stories neglected by the press, and defends working journalists when they are muzzled. The FAIR Web site will acquaint you with a variety of organizations that can help you detect media bias and let you know how you can fight the problem: *www.fair.org*.

Be an Informed Traveler

THE STATE DEPARTMENT MAKES it easy for all of us to be informed travelers by issuing official travel warnings and public announcements about potentially dangerous areas and situations as well as information packed "Consular Information Sheets" for every country in the world. The easiest, fastest, and most up-to-date way to access this information is over the Internet at *www.travel.state.gov*.

For those who don't have Internet access, the State Department offers a toll-free phone number: 1-888-407-4747, from 8:00 a.m. to 8:00 p.m. EST, Monday through Friday (except U.S. holidays). Callers who are unable to use toll-free numbers, such as those calling from overseas, can get assistance during the above mentioned hours by calling (202) 501-4444. Those who need information or assistance outside of regular business hours, including weekends and holidays, should call (202) 647-5225.

Before traveling, be sure to check the State Department for pertinent information about the areas you'll be visiting:

- **Travel Warnings** are issued whenever the State Department determines conditions are dangerous enough to recommend Americans avoid traveling to certain countries. Countries currently on the list include Iraq, Iran, Lebanon, Afghanistan, and Yemen.

- **Public Announcements** are issued any time there is a perceived threat—often one in which Americans are a specific target group. The announcements disseminate information about short-term situations such as terrorist threats, political coups, bomb threats to airlines, and anniversary dates of terrorist events.

- **Consular Information Sheets** are a quick way to learn a lot of facts about the country you plan to visit, enabling you to make more educated travel decisions. The sheets usually include locations of U.S. embassies and consulates, unusual immigration practices, health conditions, minor political disturbances, unusual currency and entry regulations, crime and security information, and drug penalties. If unstable conditions in a given country aren't severe enough to merit an official "Travel Warning," you will likely learn about the situation from the country's Consular Information Sheet. In some instances, you'll even get the same advice that's given to U.S. embassy employees.

If you don't have Internet access, you can get Consular Information Sheets by sending a self-addressed, stamped envelope to:

U.S. Department of State
American Citizens Services (Add appropriate division)
2201 C Street NW, Suite 4811
Washington, DC 20520-4818

Important: In the above address, be sure to specify the division that deals with the country you are inquiring about. The five divisions are European; African; Latin American; Near East and South Asian; and East Asian and Pacific.

STAYING HEALTHY ABROAD

Travelers not only need to protect their own health, they must also safeguard against bringing disease back to the United States—a heavy responsibility to be sure, but the Centers for Disease Control are here to help. By visiting the CDC Web site, you'll stay abreast of the latest immunization requirements and disease outbreaks that might affect travelers, as well as find a reference library of health and travel articles, tips, and resources. For those without Internet access, you can receive information by phoning toll-free 1-877-FYI-TRIP, or fax your information request to 1-888-232-3299. Otherwise, visit *www.cdc.gov.*

 Travel Emergencies

For travel-related emergencies—whether you are traveling or you urgently need to contact someone who is—call the Overseas Citizens Services 24-hour hotline at (202) 647-5225.

The State Department can also help with all kinds of problems you might encounter while abroad, including lost and stolen passports, arrests and incarceration, medical emergencies, financial assistance, and more. For a comprehensive directory of services for overseas travelers, click on *http://travel.state.gov/travel/about/who/who_1245.html.*

Three Essential Web Resources for Americans

I F YOU NEED TO find out more about the information or services offered by any government agency, one of the following three government portal Web sites will be able to point you in the right direction. The Consumer Information Center Web site (*www.pueblo.gsa.gov*) would have been in this essential list of invaluable resources, except we already covered that in the Informed Consumer chapter.

- *www.usa.gov*   Offering the most comprehensive search of government documents anywhere on the Internet, USA.gov lets you access more than 51 million Web pages from federal and state governments, the District of Columbia, and United States territories.

- *www.kids.gov*   Uncle Sam has prepared some wonderful children's Web sites on a variety of subjects. Nearly every government agency has a Web site that explains the agency's activities at a child's level: for example, see the children's sites for the FBI, CIA, Department of Treasury, Department of Labor, Department of Agriculture, and the Social Security Administration. They usually include fun and educational games, puzzles, and activities to help kids stay enthused about learning. You and your kids can access all the government's children's Web sites from this interagency kids' portal, the small-fry equivalent to government Web site portal *www.USA.gov*. Kids' Web sites can also help adults gain a quick, simple overview of a complicated subject.

- *www.defenselink.mil*   The official Web site for the Department of Defense, DefenseLink provides an excellent starting point for finding U.S. military information online.

CELEBRATE

Presidents Day

EACH YEAR, AMERICANS CELEBRATE the third Monday in February as Presidents Day, a national holiday. It wasn't always so. Prior to 1971, citizens celebrated George Washington's birthday as a federal holiday in February. Abraham Lincoln's birthday, while never designated a federal holiday, was another February holiday officially celebrated in several states. It all changed in 1971 when President Richard Nixon renamed the holiday and broadened its scope to honor *all* our past presidents. However, most citizens still think of the day as honoring Washington and Lincoln, while most car dealers and mattress stores think of the day as an excuse to have a sale.

VISIT PRESIDENTIAL LIBRARIES

A great way to celebrate Presidents Day, while learning about our more recent presidents, is to pay a visit to one of our presidential libraries. Administered by the Office of Presidential Libraries, part of the National Archives and Records Administration (NARA), these are not libraries in the traditional sense of the word. Instead they serve as museums and repositories for the documents, records, and other historic artifacts of all our presidents since Herbert Hoover.

Prior to the building of presidential libraries, presidents or their heirs decided the fate of presidential papers at the end of their administration. The Library of Congress houses some pre-Hoover collections, but others are scattered among libraries, museums, historical societies, and private collections throughout the country. Unfortunately, many of the historical artifacts and documents have been lost or even deliberately destroyed.

Franklin Roosevelt got the presidential-library ball rolling in 1939, based on his belief that presidential papers are an important part of our national heritage and that the public should have access to them. In 1955, Congress passed the Presidential Libraries Act that established a system for the libraries to be built by private donations, but maintained with federal funds and administered by NARA. While the Presidential Libraries Act "encouraged" presidents to donate their historical materials to the government, the Presidential Records Act of 1978 made it compulsory, by declaring the presidential records that document the constitutional, statutory, and ceremonial duties of the president to be the property of the U.S. government.

Exhibits using library archives to illustrate the president's life, career, and most important political achievements give visitors a deeper understanding of the man, the historical context of the times during his administration, the important policy decisions made during his presidency, and the U.S. government as a whole. Each library also offers extensive public and educational programs.

According to NARA, the 12 presidential libraries currently maintain:

- Over 400 million pages of textual materials

- Nearly 10 million photographs

- Over 15 million feet of motion picture film

- Nearly 100,000 hours of disc, audiotape, and videotape recordings

- Approximately half a million museum objects

William J. Clinton Presidential Library and Museum
1200 President Clinton Avenue
Little Rock, Arkansas 72201
(501) 374-4242
www.clintonlibrary.gov

George Bush Presidential Library and Museum
1000 George Bush Drive West
College Station, TX 77845
(979) 691-4000
http://bushlibrary.tamu.edu

Ronald Reagan Presidential Library
40 Presidential Drive
Simi Valley, CA 93065-0600
1-800-410-8354
www.reagan.utexas.edu

Jimmy Carter Library and Museum
441 Freedom Parkway
Atlanta, GA 30307-1498
(404) 865-7100
www.jimmycarterlibrary.gov

Gerald R. Ford Library
1000 Beal Avenue
Ann Arbor, MI 48109-2114
(734) 205-0555
www.fordlibrarymuseum.gov

Nixon Presidential Library and Museum
18001 Yorba Linda Boulevard
Yorba Linda, CA 92886
(714) 983-9120
www.nixonlibrary.gov

Lyndon Baines Johnson Library and Museum
2313 Red River Street
Austin, TX 78705-5702
(512) 721-0200
www.lbjlib.utexas.edu

John F. Kennedy Presidential Library and Museum
Columbia Point
Boston, MA 02125-3398
1-866-JFK-1960
www.jfklibrary.org

Dwight D. Eisenhower Presidential Library and Museum
200 Southeast Fourth Street
Abilene, KS 67410-2900
(785) 263-6700
www.eisenhowerarchives.gov

Harry S. Truman Library and Museum
500 West U.S. Highway 24
Independence, MO 64050-1798
1-800-833-1225
www.trumanlibrary.org

Franklin D. Roosevelt Presidential Library and Museum
4079 Albany Post Road
Hyde Park, NY 12538-1999
1-800-337-8474
www.fdrlibrary.marist.edu

Herbert Hoover Presidential Library and Museum
210 Parkside Drive
West Branch, IA 52358-0488
(319) 643-5301
http://hooverarchives.gov

☆ *Celebrate Presidential Proclamations*

As petitioned by Congress, or by the authority given to him in the Constitution, the president of the United States frequently issues proclamations to further the public interest. The subjects of these proclamations vary greatly—they may be designed to call the public's attention to important issues, to honor certain individuals, or to declare certain days federal holidays. Sometimes presidential proclamations have serious conse- quences, as in the Civil War when President Abraham Lincoln imposed martial law on those who gave aid and comfort to the rebels. But more often than not they're simply reasons to celebrate or to educate yourself. Recent proclamations issued by President George W. Bush include National Family Caregivers Month, Fire Prevention Week, Child Health Day, National Adoption Month, and National Preparedness Month.

You can find a comprehensive and up-to-date list of the current administration's proclamations by visiting *www.whitehouse.gov/news/proclamations.*

George Washington's Birthday

ONCE A FEDERAL HOLIDAY in its own right, George Washington's Birthday has now been incorporated into the rather generic Presidents Day celebration. Richard Nixon, who renamed the holiday in 1971, may have thought it was a good idea to honor all our presidents, but many patriotic Americans still choose to celebrate Washington's Birthday on its own day.

THE ESSENTIAL GEORGE WASHINGTON

- Born February 22, 1732, in Westmoreland County, Virginia.

- Died December 14, 1799, at Mount Vernon, Virginia.

- Commissioned as a lieutenant colonel in 1754 and fought the first skirmishes of what grew into the French and Indian War.

- Married Martha Dandridge Custis, a widow with two young children, in 1759.

- As a Virginia delegate, was elected commander in chief of the Continental Army at the Second Continental Congress in 1775.

- Forced the surrender of Cornwallis at Yorktown with the aid of French allies in 1781.

- Unanimously elected president at the Constitutional Convention of 1787.

- Took oath of office as first president of the United States April 30, 1789, standing on the balcony of Federal Hall on Wall Street in New York with John Adams serving as his vice president.

- By the end of his first term, he was disappointed that two political parties were developing. His farewell address urged his countrymen to forswear excessive party spirit and geographical distinctions and warned against long-term foreign alliances.

THE NATION'S LARGEST WASHINGTON'S BIRTHDAY CELEBRATION

Laredo, Texas, a border town of roughly 200,000 residents—about 95% of whom are Latino—serves as the unlikely host of the nation's largest celebration honoring the father of our nation. The two-week long George Washington's Birthday Festival is so big that it even spills over the border into neighboring Nuevo Laredo, Mexico.

Founded by a Laredo fraternal organization in 1898 as a way to spread international good will, the festival has become an important symbol of patriotism and civic pride to the town's residents—a place where pride in Mexican culture happily co-exists with loyal American patriotism. Good will between north and south of the border in Laredo is still celebrated at the International Bridge Ceremony where Mexican and American dignitaries exchange hugs to the musical accompaniment of both countries' national anthems. Other festivities include two parades, sporting events, great food, Tejano music, a pageant and debutante ball, and a jalapeño eating contest.

If you can't make it to Laredo on Washington's birthday, you can visit the George Washington's Birthday Celebration Museum year round. Among items on display are some of the more spectacular handmade colonial velvet and satin gowns worn throughout the years by Laredo's Martha Washington Society debutantes, some costing upwards of $25,000.

For more information about the Laredo, Texas, Washington's Birthday Celebration Association call (956) 722-0589 or visit *www.wbcalaredo.org.*

VISIT MOUNT VERNON

Eight miles south of Alexandria, Virginia, you'll find Mount Vernon, George Washington's home for over 45 years, his final resting place, and the second most visited historic home in America (the White House is first). The functional yet elegant house and grounds where Washington returned after the war to live with Martha are lovingly restored to their 1799 splendor and open for tourists 365 days a year. Visitors can also become acquainted with the innovative farming techniques and agricultural contributions our first president made to his country at Mount Vernon's fascinating Pioneer Farming exhibit. Just three miles from Mount Vernon on the site of Washington's original mill and distillery is the new George Washington's Gristmill exhibit where visitors can watch the water-powered wheel grind grain into flour just as it did 200 years ago.

Mount Vernon is open seven days a week, every day of the year, including holidays and Christmas. For additional information call (703) 780-2000 or visit *www.mountvernon.org.*

VISIT THE GEORGE WASHINGTON BIRTHPLACE NATIONAL MONUMENT

You can see the brick foundation of the house where the father of our country was born as well as the Washington family cemetery where George's father, grandfather, and great-grandfather are buried at this 550-acre park in Westmoreland County, Virginia. The historical area features the Memorial House, which depicts life in Washington's day. Picnic grounds, a nature trail, and the beautiful Potomac River beach make this an ideal location to celebrate George's birthday. Open daily from 9:00 a.m. to 5:00 p.m., except Thanksgiving, Christmas, and New Year's Day. George Washington's Birthplace is located on route 204 off route 3, 38 miles east of Fredericksburg, Virginia. For more information call (804) 224-1732 or visit *www.nps.gov/gewa*.

SEE GEORGE WASHINGTON'S DENTURES AT THE NATIONAL MUSEUM OF DENTISTRY

Home to a collection of more than 40,000 artifacts related to the history of dentistry, this Baltimore, Maryland, attraction is the proud keeper of George Washington's choppers. Contrary to folklore, the false teeth are made of ivory, not wood. The museum is located on the University of Maryland campus at 31 South Greene Street in Baltimore, Maryland. For more information call (410) 706-0600 or visit *www.dentalmuseum.org*.

ADDITIONAL INFORMATION

Read the *Papers of George Washington* online at *www.virginia.edu/gwpapers/index.html*.

UNTIL 1971, FEBRUARY 12 was observed in many states as a public holiday to honor President Abraham Lincoln's Birthday. Lincoln got short-changed in 1971 when the celebration of his birthday got rolled into the single federal public holiday, Presidents Day, observed on the third Monday of February.

But while Presidents Day honors all past presidents of the United States, there are plenty of good reasons why many Americans still choose to honor our 16th president individually. One of our most beloved leaders, Lincoln is most admired for his rise from poverty to the highest office in our land, as well as his abolishment of slavery during the Civil War.

THE ESSENTIAL ABRAHAM LINCOLN

- Born February 12, 1809, in Hardin County, Kentucky.

- Died on Good Friday, April 14, 1865, assassinated at Ford's Theatre in Washington, DC, by actor John Wilkes Booth.

- The son of a Kentucky frontiersman, grew up poor but worked hard to educate himself.

- Married Mary Todd, and fathered four sons, only one of whom lived to maturity.

- Served as a captain in the Black Hawk War.

- August 4, 1834, at 24 years old, was elected to the Illinois General Assembly as a member of the Whig Party.

- Re-elected to the Illinois General Assembly in 1836 and was, by then, a leader of the Whig Party.

- Received his license to practice law on September 9, 1836.

- Lost an 1858 Senate election to Stephen A. Douglas, but gained national attention as a great debater.

- Elected our first Republican president in 1860, and received 180 of 303 possible electoral votes and 40 percent of the popular vote.

- As president, helped build the Republican Party into a strong national organization.

- Issued the Emancipation Proclamation on January 1, 1863, freeing all slaves held in Confederate Territories.

- Won re-election in 1864, defeating Democrat George B. McClellan and earning 212 of 233 electoral votes and 55 percent of the popular vote.

- Laid to rest in Oak Ridge Cemetery, outside Springfield, Illinois.

VISIT LINCOLN'S BOYHOOD HOME

The National Park Service maintains the 228-acre Abraham Lincoln Boyhood Home at Knob Creek in LaRue County, Kentucky. Also nearby, south of Hodgenville, Kentucky, you'll find the Abraham Lincoln Birthplace National Historic Site. Each year on the second Saturday in October during Lincoln Days, lots of "Honest Abes" show up to compete in a look-alike contest and march in the Lincoln Days Parade in Hodgenville. Throughout the year, Lincoln impersonators perform first-person living history impressions in towns all across the United States. For more information, contact the Kentucky Department of Travel at 1-800-225-8747 or visit *www.kytourism.com*.

VISIT THE LINCOLN MUSEUM

The world's largest museum dedicated to the life and times of Abraham Lincoln, the Lincoln Museum interprets and preserves the history and legacy of Abraham Lincoln through research, preservation, exhibits, and education. The museum's library houses nearly 18,000 published volumes and thousands of manuscripts, including over 300 original Lincoln documents. The Lincoln Museum is located at 200 East Berry Street, Fort Wayne, Indiana 46802. Their phone number is (260) 455-3864 and their Web site is *www.thelincolnmuseum.org*.

VISIT FORD'S THEATRE

Ford's Theatre, where Abraham Lincoln was assassinated on April 14, 1865, now serves as a National Historic Site. Among items on display in the theatre's basement museum are the clothes Lincoln wore on his final night, the death-delivering pistol that was used to shoot him, and the flag that draped his coffin. Visitors will also find the theatre's presidential box, where the Lincolns sat on that fateful evening, restored to its original condition. Ford's Theatre is located at 511 10th Street, Washington, DC. The museum is open from 9 a.m. to 5 p.m. daily, except Christmas. For more information call (202) 426-6924 or visit *www.nps.gov/foth*.

Martin Luther King Jr.'s Birthday

EACH YEAR ON THE third Monday of January, America celebrates and honors the life, work, and dream of slain civil rights leader Dr. Martin Luther King Jr. The only American besides George Washington to have a national holiday designated for his birthday, Dr. King is also one of the few social leaders in the world to be so honored.

Creating a new federal holiday in the United States is no easy matter. Holidays have a large fiscal impact on taxpayers, as they give federal employees a paid day off. Countless groups constantly lobby Congress to honor a multitude of heroes. Elected officials must walk a delicate political tightrope in choosing who does and does not merit their own special day.

Despite the challenges presented to them, the Southern Christian Leadership Conference felt so strongly about Dr. King's message of nonviolent social change, that they worked diligently on the cause of creating a holiday in his honor. Coordinating over 6 million signatures—one of the largest petition drives in history—and submitting them to Congress in 1970, the Conference applied continuous pressure during an arduous 15- year lobbying effort. It finally paid off when Ronald Reagan signed the legislation that created the holiday in 1983.

THE ESSENTIAL MARTIN LUTHER KING JR.

- Born January 15, 1929, at his family home, 501 Auburn Avenue, NE, Atlanta, Georgia.

- Died April 4, 1968, shot by an assassin's bullet in Memphis, Tennessee, where he was working to help lead sanitation workers in a protest against low wages and intolerable working conditions.

- Entered Morehouse College at the age of 15, graduated in 1948 with a B.A. degree in sociology.

- Ordained a Christian minister at Ebenezer Baptist Church in Atlanta, Georgia, at the age of 19. Although he would leave this post for periods of time during his life, he returned from 1960 until his death in 1968 and served as co-pastor of Ebenezer Baptist Church with his father.

- Married Coretta Scott on June 18, 1953.

- Fathered four children: two girls and two boys.

- Enrolled in Crozer Theological Seminary in Chester, Pennsylvania, and simultaneously studied at the University of Pennsylvania. He was elected president of the senior class at Crozer, delivered the valedictory address, won the Peral Plafkner Award as the most outstanding student, and received the J. Lewis Crozer Fellowship for graduate study at a university of his choice. Awarded a Bachelor of Divinity degree from Crozer in 1951.

- Began doctoral studies in systematic theology at Boston University, and was awarded his Ph.D. on June 5, 1955.

- Elected president of the Montgomery Improvement Association. Under his leadership the organization was responsible for the successful Montgomery, Alabama, Bus Boycott from 1955 to 1956.

- Returned to Atlanta in 1959 to direct the activities of the Southern Christian Leadership Conference.

- A pivotal figure in the civil rights movement, Dr. King was arrested 30 times for his participation in civil rights activities.

- Won the Nobel Peace Prize in 1964 at the age of 35. Dr. King was the youngest man, the second American, and the third black man to ever be honored with the prestigious award.

VISIT THE KING CENTER AND THE MARTIN LUTHER KING JR. NATIONAL HISTORIC SITE

Established in 1968 by Dr. King's widow, the late Coretta Scott King, the King Center is the official memorial dedicated to the advancement of the legacy of Dr. Martin Luther King Jr. More than 650,000 visitors annually visit the center to pay homage to Dr. King, view exhibits illustrating his life and teachings, and visit the King Center Library, Dr. King's final resting place, his birth home, and Ebenezer Baptist Church, where he worked for many years.

Tours of the King Center and the National Martin Luther King Jr. Historic Site are self-guided and free of charge. Tickets are required to tour the King Birth Home; you can get them at the Visitor's Center, where they are issued on a first-come, first-served basis. To avoid disappointment, pick up your tickets early in the day as tours are limited to 15 visitors per group. Facilities are open from 9:00 a.m. to 5:00 p.m. daily (with extended summer hours for some attractions). All King Center exhibits, tours, and shops are closed on Christmas Day and Thanksgiving Day.

Call (404) 526-8900 for King Center information and (404) 331-5190 for tour information. The King Center is located just east of downtown Atlanta, Georgia. The Web site is *www.thekingcenter.org*.

Memorial Day

IN 1866, AS THE United States was recovering from a long and bloody civil war, Henry Welles, a drugstore owner in Waterloo, New York, had the idea that all the shops in town should close for one day to honor the Union soldiers buried there. And so it came to pass that on the morning of May 5, the townspeople decorated the graves of the soldiers with flowers, wreaths, and crosses. At roughly the same time period, Retired Major General Jonathan A. Logan planned another ceremony in Waterloo called Decoration Day, honoring soldiers who had survived the war. Veterans marched through town to the cemetery to adorn their compatriots' graves with flags. The two ceremonies joined forces in 1868.

By 1882, Decoration Day became known as Memorial Day and the tribute extended to soldiers who had died in all previous wars. In 1966, President Lyndon Johnson proclaimed Waterloo the birthplace of Memorial Day, 100 years after the first celebration. In 1971, President Richard Nixon declared Memorial Day a federal holiday to be celebrated on the last Monday in May.

MEMORIAL DAY AT ARLINGTON

The nation's largest national cemetery, Arlington, provides an especially poignant location to observe Memorial Day. On the Friday morning before Memorial Day, soldiers of the Third U.S. infantry walk along the rows of Arlington's headstones, stopping to place a small American flag next to each veteran's grave.

You'll also find the Tomb of the Unknowns at Arlington, which actually housed four graves until 1998: one from each of the World Wars, one from the Korean Conflict, and one from the Vietnam War. In 1998 DNA testing identified the remains of the Vietnam serviceperson buried in the Tomb of the Unknowns as United States Air Force First Lieutenant Michael Joseph Blassie. His remains were returned to his family and were buried in his hometown of St. Louis, Missouri. It has been decided that the crypt that formerly held the remains of the Vietnam Unknown will remain vacant. Guarded year round, 24 hours a day, by soldiers from the Army's Third Infantry, on Memorial Day the president or vice president gives a speech and lays a wreath on the tomb. Armed forces members shoot a rifle salute into the air in solemn tribute.

HONOR VETERANS AT NATIONAL CEMETERIES AROUND THE COUNTRY

On July 17, 1862, President Lincoln signed legislation authorizing the federal government to buy land for use as national cemeteries "for soldiers who shall have died in the service of the country." Until then, those lost in battle were usually buried in fields and church-yards close to the hospitals, battlefields, and prison camps where they died.

After the Civil War, army crews tried to locate, exhume, and rebury deceased Union soldiers in our original 14 national cemeteries. The need for space was vastly underestimated as the five-year reinterment process necessitated the building of 50 more cemeteries. The original national cemeteries also became the final resting place of many Confederate prisoners of war who were buried with honor, although Congress wouldn't approve paying to mark their graves with headstones until 1906.

Eventually, our national cemeteries expanded their reach to welcome all veterans of the United States armed forces, American war veterans of allied forces, as well as veterans' spouses and dependent children. Those eligible for burial in a national cemetery are given a gravesite and headstone or marker. The Veteran's Administration makes sure the graves are perpetually cared for at no cost to the veteran's family or heirs.

Our national cemeteries offer ample opportunities for Americans to honor our deceased military on Memorial Day or any time of year. Covering more than 17,000 acres of land from Hawaii to Maine, and from Alaska to Puerto Rico, more than 300 recipients of the Medal of Honor are buried in our national cemeteries. For a listing of all the U.S. national and veterans' cemeteries, visit *www.interment.net/us/nat/veterans.htm*.

FLAG ETIQUETTE

American flags should be flown at half-mast on Memorial Day to honor our lost veterans.

☆ *Why Wear Poppies?*

The wearing of small paper poppies known as "Buddy Poppies" has been a patriotic Memorial Day tradition since 1923. Made by disabled and aging veterans in VA Hospitals and homes across the country, the poppies provide money to assist the veterans and their families.

Sold by local Veterans of Foreign Wars (VFW) posts, Buddy Poppy proceeds do not profit any VFW unit, but rather go directly to help veterans in need. The VFW was granted all trademark rights to the name "Buddy Poppy" in 1924, which means no other organization or individual can use that name. The "Buddy Poppy" label provides the public a way of knowing they are getting the real deal.

So why poppies? The tradition stems from John McCrae's 1915 war poem "In Flanders Field," which speaks of the poppy covered Flanders Field U.S. military cemetery in Belgium, where the bodies of 368 World War I veterans are buried. It seems poppies only grow in rooted up soil, and because of the war, the soil had been churned to such a degree that poppies bloomed in abundance. This is the sight that greeted poet McCrae at Flanders Field and the rest is history.

ADDITIONAL INFORMATION

- Full history of the VFW's Buddy Poppies Program is found at *www.vfw.org*.

- Donate to the VFW at *https://secure2.convio.net/vfw/site/SPage Server?pagename=donation_main*.

Have a Safe and Happy Independence Day

NOTHING QUITE STIRS PATRIOTIC feelings like a dazzling display of fireworks on the Fourth of July. But used improperly, fireworks can turn a festive holiday into tragedy. The good news is that legal fireworks are safer than ever, in part because of stringent federal safety standards enacted by the U.S. Consumer Product Safety Commission in time for our nation's 1976 bicentennial. The incidence of fireworks-related injuries has dropped dramatically during the past 10 years, according to the National Council on Fireworks Safety, a nonprofit organization dedicated to the safe enjoyment of fireworks in the United States. The council offers these simple suggestions to help make your holiday safer:

- Use only legal fireworks. The Consumer Product Safety Commission requires that legal fireworks show the name of the item, the name of the manufacturer or distributor, and easy-to-read cautionary labeling and instructions for proper use. Illegal fireworks are usually unlabeled, do not bear a caution statement, and often do not list the manufacturer's name.

- Always purchase fireworks from reliable sources.

- A responsible adult should supervise all fireworks activities.

- Never give fireworks to children.

- Follow label directions carefully.

- Never point or throw fireworks at another person.

- Use fireworks outdoors in a clear area away from buildings and vehicles.

- Never carry fireworks in your pocket or shoot them in metal or glass containers.

- Light fireworks one at a time, then move back quickly.

- Don't experiment with homemade fireworks.

- Observe local laws and use common sense.

- Sparklers, fountains, and other items that many states allow for use by consumers are not appropriate when a large crowd is present.

ADDITIONAL INFORMATION

The National Council on Fireworks Safety Web site offers tips on choosing fireworks, fireworks safety, state laws restricting fireworks use, plus news and resources: *www.fireworksafety.com*.

Find federal fireworks regulations as well as more safety tips in English and Spanish from our government's Consumer Product Safety Commission (CPSC) at *www.cpsc.gov/cpscpub/pubs/july4/4thjuly.html*.

The CPSC's fireworks safety Web site for kids is at *cpsc.gov/kids/kidsafety/kiddfwks.html*.

Honor Veterans on Veterans Day

THE HOLIDAY WE NOW celebrate as Veterans Day originally went by another name. In 1938, Congress declared the 11th of

November a day to be dedicated to the cause of world peace and to be known as "Armistice Day."

In 1954, after World War II, Congress amended the Act of 1938 by substituting the word "Veterans" for the word "Armistice," at the urging of several veterans' service organizations. Where Armistice Day celebrated World War I vets, the new holiday set aside time to honor *all* veterans. And so it came about that on October 8, 1954, President Dwight D. Eisenhower issued the first Veterans Day Proclamation.

A lot of people don't understand the difference between Memorial Day and Veterans Day. Memorial Day honors and remembers military personnel who died in service to their country. Veterans Day is set aside to honor *everyone* who honorably served in the military—in times of war or peace, living or deceased. In fact, Veterans Day provides an excellent opportunity for Americans to honor and thank the men and women who currently protect our nation.

WHEN IS VETERANS DAY?

Confusion abounds about when to celebrate Veterans Day. It comes as a result of the "Uniform Monday Holiday Act," signed in 1968. This law gave federal employees three-day weekends off for Washington's Birthday, Memorial Day, Veterans Day, and Columbus Day, regardless of which day of the week the holiday actually fell (and in 1983, Martin Luther King Jr.'s Birthday was added to the list). But in 1978 Congress restored the observance of Veterans Day to its original November 11 date, and the Veterans Day National Ceremony, like most around the nation, is celebrated on the actual day. (Federal employees are still granted a Monday holiday for Veterans Day if November 11 falls on a weekend though.)

VETERAN'S REUNIONS

Do you know a veteran who would love to connect with an old military buddy? Military reunions for thousands of outfits go on all the time. The best way to find out about them is via the Internet. The following Web sites list information for over 12,000 different reunions, as well as offer advice on how to find old military buddies and how to organize your own reunions.

- Military Connections.com has over 450,000 active duty, reserve, war veterans, and retired military personnel in their database. See if your buddies are among them at *www.militaryconnections.com.*

- VetFinders.com also keeps a database (over 200,000 and growing) of military personnel seeking to reconnect with old acquaintances: *www.VetFinders.com.*

- The National Personnel Records Center is the repository of millions of military personnel, health, and medical records of discharged and deceased veterans of all services during the 20th century. They also store medical treatment records of retirees from all services, as well as records for dependent and other persons treated at naval medical facilities. Information from the records is made available upon written request (with signature and date) to the extent allowed by law. Call (314) 801-0800, or go to *www.archives.gov/st-louis/military-personnel.*

ADDITIONAL INFORMATION

Get the schedule for national Veterans Day events at the Department of Veteran's Affairs Veterans Day Page: *www.va.gov/vetsday/index.cfm.*

⭐ *Attractions to Celebrate and Honor America's Veterans*

What better way to honor and appreciate America's veterans than to understand the importance of why they fought? Numerous museums, monuments, and historical sites around the country provide wonderful opportunities to learn more about the causes our nation has fought for throughout its history, and honor the heroes who bravely gave their lives to protect our country. Here are three outstanding examples:

National Vietnam Veterans Memorial   One of the most visited sites in Washington, DC, the Vietnam Veterans Memorial provides a moving tribute to the sacrifice made by American military personnel during one of our country's most unpopular wars. The Memorial seeks to pave the way to a healing process between the political issues of those who opposed the war and those who valiantly served their country. Built through private donations from the public, three components make up the memorial: the Wall of Names, honoring those who died in Vietnam; the Three Servicemen Statue and Flagpole; and the Vietnam Women's Memorial. Find the Memorial at Bacon Drive and Constitution Avenue in Washington, DC. The Foggy Bottom Metro Stop will get you there. The public may visit the site 24 hours a day, although rangers will be there to answer questions between the hours of 9:30 a.m. and 11:30 p.m. daily. Call (202) 426-6841 for more information or visit *www.nps.gov/vive/index.htm*.

The National Museum of the Pacific War   Fredericksburg, Texas, the boyhood home of World War II hero Admiral Chester

W. Nimitz, is the site of the only museum in the continental United States dedicated exclusively to telling the story of the Pacific Theater battles of World War II. The seven-acre museum site includes the George Bush Gallery, the Admiral Nimitz Museum, Veterans' Walk of Honor, and the Japanese Garden of Peace—a gift of good will and healing from the military leaders of Japan to the people of the United States. These and other compelling exhibits and presentations really create a deeper and more meaningful understanding of the triumphs and tragedies of this important historical period. The National Museum of the Pacific War is located at 340 East Main Street in Fredericksburg, Texas. It's open every day, except Christmas and Thanksgiving, from 9 a.m. to 5:00 p.m. Allow at least $1\frac{1}{2}$ to 2 hours to tour all of the facilities. For more information, call (830) 997-4379 or visit *www.nimitz-museum.org*.

U.S.S. *Arizona* Memorial   A navy-operated launch boat transports visitors to Honolulu, Hawaii's U.S.S. *Arizona* Memorial. Built over the remains of the sunken battleship downed by Japanese navy bombs on December 7, 1941, the 184-foot-long Memorial structure commemorates the worst naval disaster in American History. It also serves as the dramatic final resting place for many of the 1,177 crewmen killed during the attack. A marble wall engraved with the names of the dead really puts the enormous loss of the "Day of Infamy" into shocking perspective. The U.S.S. *Arizona* Memorial tour program consists of a brief introduction given by a park ranger, Pearl Harbor survivor, or volunteer, followed by a 23-minute documentary film on the history of Pearl Harbor. A short boat ride then transports visitors to the actual memorial. The entire program takes about an hour and 15 minutes. Tours are free and offered on a first-come, first-served basis. Peak season wait times can exceed two hours, so plan to arrive at the visitor center no later than 12:00 p.m. during busy times of year. The memorial is open daily from 7:30 a.m. to 5:00 p.m., except Thanksgiving, Christmas, and New Year's Day. Interpretive programs and boat trips begin at 8:00 a.m. (7:45 a.m. in summer). The last program each day begins at 3:00 p.m. Due to the terrorist attacks on the United States and the location of the USS *Arizona* Memorial on an active military base, strict security measures are currently being enforced. That means no purses, handbags, fanny packs, backpacks, camera bags, diaper bags, luggage, or other items that offer concealment are allowed in the visitor center or on the memorial. Strollers with pockets and compartments must be empty before being allowed in the visitor center. Personal cameras are okay. For visitor information, call (808) 422-0561 or visit *www.nps.gov/usar/index.htm*.

Arbor Day

TREES PROVIDE OXYGEN; FOOD for both animals and people; wood for building products, paper, and fuel; and windbreaks that hold soil in place, not to mention cooling shade on hot summer days. But Nebraska in the early 1870s was a vast plain barren of trees, which prompted J. Sterling Morton, editor of the state's first newspaper, the *Nebraska City News*, to advocate tree planting by individuals as well as civic groups.

Morton first proposed a tree-planting holiday at a meeting of the State Board of Agriculture in 1872. Prizes were offered to the counties who planted the largest number of trees. Morton's holiday was a great success as it was estimated that more than 1 million trees took root in Nebraska on our country's first Arbor Day.

During the 1870s, other states jumped on the bandwagon, passing legislation to observe Arbor Day. Today the event is officially celebrated on the last Friday in April, although many states observe Arbor Day on different dates, depending upon their best tree-planting times. Schools, civic organizations, and individuals take part each year by planting trees and nurturing the environment.

WHY PLANTING TREES IS GOOD FOR AMERICA

According to the U.S. Department of Agriculture, the net cooling effect of a young, healthy tree is equivalent to 10 room-size air conditioners operating 20 hours a day.

- The Department of Agriculture also reports that one acre of forest absorbs six tons of carbon dioxide and puts out four tons of oxygen, enough to meet the annual needs of 18 people.

- The USDA Forest Service says trees properly placed around buildings can reduce air-conditioning needs by 30 percent and can save 20 to 50 percent in the energy used for heating.

- The planting of trees results in improved water quality and less runoff and erosion. Wooded areas help prevent the transport of sediment and chemicals into streams.

- Healthy, mature trees can add an average of 10 percent to a property's value, say the Forest Service statistics.

Join the National Arbor Day Foundation and get 10 free trees! You'll also find a state by state listing of Arbor Day celebration dates. Contact the National Arbor Day Foundation, 100 Arbor Avenue, Nebraska City, NE 68410; (402) 474-5655; *www.arborday.org*.

American Forests, an organization which has worked to protect trees since 1875, has an easy way for Americans to help plant trees. In fact, you can decide exactly where your American Forests donations go. The South Texas Wildlife Refuge, California Wildfire ReLeaf, and Katrina ReLeaf Fund offer but a few of the tree- planting opportunities awaiting concerned Americans. Get more information at *www.americanforests.org*.

Visit Our Nation's Capital— Tips for Touring DC

USE YOUR CONNECTIONS AND GET
SPECIAL CONGRESSIONAL TOURS

DID YOU KNOW THAT your state senator or congressional representative's office can be your key to obtaining special Congressional Guided Tour tickets for the White House, Supreme Court, U.S. Capitol, and the National Archives buildings? The free tours usually leave early in the morning, before regular tours begin. Small size and attentive, knowledgeable guides make Congressional Tours more comprehensive and compelling than their general public counterparts.

Keep in mind the small monthly ticket allotment given to each representative's office tends to go quickly. Contact your representative's local or Washington headquarters several months in advance of your trip to ensure success in obtaining tickets.

Your political public servants also can and will get you passes to watch Congress in session. Check the Senate and House calendars before requesting passes so you'll know which days Congress is in session and in recess. *The Washington Post's* daily calendar will keep you up-to-date with congressional times and topics for discussion.

Most representatives have additional information about these services and touring Washington, DC, in general posted on their Web sites.

SELF-GUIDED TOURS OF THE WHITE HOUSE

Public tours of the White House are available for groups of 10 or more people. Requests must be submitted through one's Member of Congress and are accepted up to six months in advance. The self-guided tours are available from 7:30 a.m. to 12:30 p.m. Tuesday through Saturday (excluding federal holidays), and are scheduled on a first-come, first-served basis approximately one month in advance of the requested date. You should submit your request as early as possible since only a limited number of tours are available. Even confirmed reservations are no guarantee as White House tours may be subject to last minute cancellation. For the most current tour information call the 24-hour information line at (202) 456-7041 or go to *www.whitehouse.gov/history/tours*.

EXPERIENCING THE SUPREME COURT

The Supreme Court is open to the public from 9 a.m. to 4:30 p.m., Monday through Friday. Between 9:30 a.m. and 3:30 p.m., free lectures about the court are given to the public every hour on the half hour. Tours begin in the courtroom when the court is not in session. When court is in session, tours are offered only on Thursdays and Fridays and no tours are given in August. The public is also invited to witness the Supreme Court in action beginning the first Monday in October and continuing until late April. Oral arguments are conducted on Mondays, Tuesdays, and Wednesdays from 10:00 a.m. to 2:00 p.m. First-come, first-served seating is limited, so arrive early. Call (202) 479-3000 for further information on visiting the Supreme Court or visit *www.supremecourtus.gov/visiting/visiting.html*.

VISITING THE CAPITOL

General visiting hours are from 9:00 a.m. to 4:30 p.m., Monday through Saturday. Because of security concerns as well as Capitol Visitor Center construction, times and visitor restrictions can frequently change, so you should always call the Capitol Guide Service Recorded Information Line at (202) 225-6827 before visiting. Contact your senators or representatives well in advance of visiting to obtain passes to view congress in session. For more information about visiting the Capitol go to *www.aoc.gov*.

TOURING THE BUREAU OF ENGRAVING AND PRINTING

Because of security concerns, tour information and availability changes frequently, so visitors should always call the tour office at (202) 874-2330 or toll-free 1-866-874-2330 for updated opening and closing information. You can also get timely details from *www.bep.treas.gov/locations/index.cfm/3*.

EXPLORING THE NATIONAL ARCHIVES

The Rotunda of the National Archives Building in downtown Washington, DC, displays the Constitution, the Bill of Rights, and the Declaration of Independence. The building is open for tourists from 10 a.m. to 7 p.m. March 15 through Labor Day and from 10 a.m. to 5:30 p.m. after Labor Day until March 14. Last admission is 30 minutes prior to closing. The National Archives is closed Thanksgiving Day and Christmas Day. Call the NARA opening-status line at (301) 837-0700 for the latest on openings and closings. For more information visit *www.archives.gov/dc-metro/washington/index.html*.

INVESTIGATING THE FBI

Because of security concerns, all tours of FBI headquarters have been suspended. As of this printing, no time is scheduled for tours to resume. Check the FBI's Web site for any possible changes: *www.fbi.gov*.

THE HEART AND SOUL OF WASHINGTON, DC

If you want to discover DC beyond the obvious tourist attractions, the DC Heritage Tourism Coalition can help. A joint effort of people who manage the city's museums, cultural attractions, and neighborhood organizations, the coalition is united by the common mission of encouraging DC tourists to discover the rich history and cultural points of interest beyond the monuments. The coalition is currently focusing on new ways for tourists to enjoy the nation's capital, including bus and walking tours, heritage trails, and special interest, self-guided themed itineraries. These self-guided tours allow visitors to discover the parts of the city that most interest them, from art and architecture to historic homes and African American heritage. For more information, call the DC Heritage Tourism Coalition at (202) 661-7581or visit *www.dcheritage.org.*

METRO

Washington's subway system provides an excellent way to explore the city. Beautiful, efficient, clean, and fun, the METRO system links all parts of Washington with the nearby Virginia and Maryland suburbs. For a great travel bargain, check out METRO's convenient one-day visitor's pass, allowing unlimited, all-day travel on the system. For more information on how to get around, visit the Washington Metropolitan Area Transit Authority Web site at *www.wmata.com* or call (202) 962-1234.

DRIVING IN DC

Parking is restricted during rush hours and during some weekend hours. Read all signs carefully and don't try to "get away with it" by parking illegally—you will get ticketed and in many cases, towed. During rush hour, certain major arteries change in favor of rush hour traffic. Pay close attention to street signs.

ADDITIONAL INFORMATION

- The Washington, DC, Convention and Visitors Association sponsors the official Washington, DC, tourism Web site: *www.washington.org.* Phone is 1-800-422-8644; address is 1212 New York Avenue NW, Suite 600, Washington, DC 20005.

- Official Washington, DC, homepage is at *www.dchomepage.net.*

Visit the Statue of Liberty and Ellis Island ★

LIBERTY ENLIGHTENING THE WORLD, or the Statue of Liberty as she is better known, has proudly welcomed visitors to New York harbor since 1886. America's second most famous patriotic symbol (after the flag), the statue holds special significance for the more than 12 million immigrants who first spotted this icon of hope and freedom after long and arduous journeys that culminated at the processing center at nearby Ellis Island.

The trip to either of these attractions begins by catching a Circle Line ferry in Battery Park on the southern tip of Manhattan or at Liberty Park in New Jersey. Aside from food and souvenirs, the ferry fee is the only charge for visiting the Statue of Liberty or Ellis Island. Ferries run about every 30 to 45 minutes beginning at 8:30 a.m. (later in the off season). Crowds are generally smaller earlier in the day, especially during the busy summer months. To get the best photo or video shots, try to sit on the right side of the boat after leaving Battery Park and on the left side when returning. For ticket rates and schedule information, call (212) 269-5755 or book your tickets online at *www.StatueReservations.com*.

TOURING THE STATUE OF LIBERTY

Visitors wanting to go to the top of the statue must choose between two options: take an elevator located in the center of the statue or make a 22-story climb that wraps around the interior and up the sides. The latter, while physically challenging, is well worth the effort as it allows views of the statue's fascinating inner iron skeleton. The climb is by far the most popular way to tour the statue, and the wait to mount the steps can sometimes top two to three hours during the spring and fall peak seasons. The ascent involves some tricky steps on winding, spiral staircases so it's a good idea to wear sturdy, rubber-soled shoes.

The National Park Service offers outdoor tours of the statue area from April 1 through October 31. Indoor Museum tours run from November 1 through March 31. The 30-minute tours are offered on a first-come, first-served basis with availability dependent on current staffing levels.

STATUE OF LIBERTY FACTS AND TRIVIA

- Construction of the statue began in France in 1875 and was completed in June 1884.

- Lady Liberty was dismantled and shipped to United States in early 1885.

- The sculptor was Auguste Bartholdi.

- The structural engineer was Gustave Eiffel (of Eiffel Tower fame).

- The architect of the pedestal was Richard Morris Hunt.

- On October 28, 1886, President Grover Cleveland officially accepted the statue on behalf of the United States as a gift from France.

- The Statue of Liberty was officially designated a national monument on October 15, 1924.

- Until 1956, Liberty Island was called Bedloe's Island.

- The original torch is on display in the statue's base. The one that now lights New York Harbor was put into place during the statue's extensive 1980s renovation.

- The statue's 10-foot-wide head gives visitors a spectacular 180-degree view

- At one time the public was allowed to climb up a ladder inside the arm, but safety precautions now prohibit that activity.

- The book in Liberty's arm reads "July 4, 1776" in roman numerals.

VISITING ELLIS ISLAND

Ellis Island served as the gateway for more than half of the immigrants entering the United States between 1892 and 1924. During the height of the immigration influx, as many as 10,000 people would file through Ellis Island in a single 24-hour period.

The island stood empty from 1954 until 1965 when President Lyndon Johnson added it to the Statue of Liberty National Monument under the jurisdiction of the National Park Service. The Island was again closed to public tours from 1980 until it reopened in 1990 after a $160 million restoration, which included the opening of the 200,000 square foot Ellis Island Immigration Museum. The tour is self-guided, but it's a good idea to rent an audio-tour to get the most out of your museum visit.

THE AMERICAN IMMIGRANT WALL OF HONOR
AT ELLIS ISLAND

Be sure to look at the American Immigrant Wall of Honor, which displays the names of countless people who risked everything to come to America. Offering an especially moving tribute to the men and women who helped build our nation, the names were inscribed on the wall by the children, grandchildren, and great grandchildren of these courageous immigrants. The Wall of Honor serves as a constant reminder of and tribute to the courageous travelers who dared to follow their dreams to a new land.

The Immigrant Wall of Honor is the only national monument where any American can have a name inscribed in tribute. If you'd like to honor an immigrant relative, call (212) 561-4500 for more information or write:

> Ellis Campaign
> 292 Madison Avenue
> New York, NY 10017-7769

TRACE YOUR IMMIGRANT HISTORY ONLINE

Genealogy has become one of the most popular American hobbies. For many Americans, there's no better place to start the search for information about their family's past than Ellis Island. It's estimated that more than 40 percent of all U.S. citizens can trace their ancestry back to an immigrant who entered the country through the Ellis Island processing center.

In the digital age, the Statue of Liberty–Ellis Island Foundation has made it easy to trace your ancestors online by cataloging the immigration records of the Ellis Island Immigrant Processing Center. A simple search of my maternal grandparents' names instantly brought up my mother's, grandmother's, aunt's, and uncle's Ellis Island immigration records. Isn't the Internet amazing! Trace your family's history by visiting *www.ellisislandrecords.org*.

⭐ ### *Pennsylvania Museum Shows the World "Through Immigrant Eyes"*

One of Johnstown, Pennsylvania's best attractions, the Johnstown Heritage Discovery Center offers visitors a chance to see the world as a typical Ellis Island immigrant might have. Not content to be a "look at artifacts behind the glass" type of museum, Discovery Center visitors actually participate in an innovative interactive adventure. The museum makes the American immigrant experience of the early 1900s personal and emotionally compelling in a way that books or more stagnant exhibits simply can't equal, for children and adults alike.

Upon entering the center, guests are asked to choose a bar-coded character card. The eight characters represent different ages and ethnic backgrounds, but their stories are similar to the millions of immigrants who came to America in the early 1900s, seeking a better life. While walking through the museum, you'll experience, interactively, some of the most important events that happened to your character.

Your journey begins with the recreation of an intimidating encounter with an Ellis Island immigration officer. You'll then follow your character and deal with issues like finding employment, and coping with the day-to-day prejudices and hardships as well as celebrating the joy of ethnic life in 1907. Authentic sets, historic photos, and multimedia exhibits provide the look and feel of the era, including homes, shops, and places of worship.

The memories taken away from the Heritage Center will be different for each member of the family, depending on the character cards chosen. Your family will no doubt have a lot to talk about when comparing notes afterward, as everyone leaves with a computer printout summary of how their character's life turned out.

The Heritage Discovery Center is located at Broad Street and 7th Avenue in Johnstown, Pennsylvania, and is open Monday through Friday from 10 a.m. to 5 p.m. and from 10 a.m. to 7 p.m. on Saturday and Sunday in peak season. For more information call the Johnstown Area Heritage Association at (814) 539-1889. You can also visit their Web site at *www.ja ha.org.*

Visit Our National Parks

OUR NATIONAL PARKS PROVIDE over 272 million annual visitors with endless recreational opportunities, as well as the chance to learn about important American historical events and to bask in nature's majestic glory. Today, the National Park Service administers 391 park areas, encompassing approximately 84 million acres.

When most people think of our national parks, they think of places like Yellowstone, Yosemite, or the Grand Canyon, but the Park Service also includes historic monuments, battlefields, cemeteries, rivers, nature preserves, and more. At 13,200,000 acres, Wrangell-St. Elias National Park and Preserve in Alaska is the Park Service's largest property, while Pennsylvania's Thaddeus Kosciuszko National Memorial is the smallest, at 0.02 acre.

Three main classifications categorize the Park Service properties: natural areas, historical areas, and recreational areas, although to be sure, some parks represent all three. The various types of properties under the administration of our National Park Service include:

National Parks   National parks are generally large, unspoiled properties offering spectacular scenery and sometimes significant historic assets. To preserve the pristine beauty of our national parks, activities such as hunting, mining, or anything else that might disrupt the delicate ecology of the land are strictly prohibited.

National Preserves   A close relative of the national parks, national preserves are nearly identical in character except that Congress does allow public hunting and trapping, as well as oil and gas exploration and extraction and mining on national preserve lands.

National Recreation Areas   Twelve of our national recreation areas are located on large reservoirs and emphasize water-based recreation. Urban parks that provide city dwellers with some much needed outdoor recreation space account for the remaining national recreation areas.

National Seashores   Ten national seashores dot the coasts of the Atlantic, Gulf of Mexico, and Pacific. Some are developed for tourism, but others remain primitive.

National Lakeshores   All of our national lakeshores can be found around the Great Lakes, and like our national seashores, some are developed for tourism while others remain in their natural state.

National Rivers   Within this category, you'll find several subcategories including national river and recreation areas accessible for public use as well as national scenic rivers and wild rivers.

National Monuments The Antiquities Act of 1906 gave the president the authority to make public proclamations making "national monuments" of landmarks, structures, and other objects of historic or scientific interest situated on lands owned or controlled by the government. The Statue of Liberty is our most famous national monument.

National Historic Sites National historic sites usually highlight a single historical event.

National Historical Parks A step beyond historic sites, historic parks generally encompass larger areas or groups of buildings with historic significance.

National Memorials National memorials honor the life of an historic person or historic event. They may or may not occupy an actual site associated with that person or event. Mount Rushmore is a well-known example.

National Battlefields Battlefields commemorate the site of a significant historical battle.

National Cemeteries National cemeteries serve as the final resting places for scores of America's military men and women.

National Parkways Often used to connect important historical sites, national parkways provide scenic road trips along protected corridors.

National Trails Over 3,600 miles of linear parklands are at Americans' disposal for hiking, biking, horseback riding, cross-country skiing, snowshoeing, and snowmobiling.

Affiliated Areas   The affiliated areas, while technically outside the national parks system, do receive financial or technical help from the Service, as our government has recognized them as being important enough to preserve.

GET A NATIONAL PARKS PASS

The National Parks Pass provides holders with admission for an entire year to any and all national parks charging an entrance fee. As of this writing, the pass costs just $80 and over 80 percent of the proceeds from the sales of National Parks Passes go directly to support our parks. In today's tough economy, the passes represent a genuine travel bargain as one pass admits an entire extended family—spouses, children, and grandparents. If the park charges a per vehicle fee, your National Parks Pass admits you along with everyone else in your car.

You can purchase a National Parks Pass:

- At the gate to any national park where an entrance fee is charged.
- At participating park bookstores operated by cooperating associations.
- Online at *http://store.usgs.gov/pass*.
- By phone at 1-888-ASK-USGS.

Note: A National Parks Pass does not cover camping fees.

"GOLDEN" PASSPORTS

If you are a U.S. citizen or permanent resident age 62 or older, the Golden Age Passport admits you, your spouse, and your children to national parks, monuments, historic sites, recreation areas, and national wildlife refuges for the rest of your life. The Golden Access Passport offers identical benefits for blind or permanently disabled citizens and permanent residents. Both "Golden" passports also give their holders a 50 percent discount on federal use fees charged for camping, swimming, parking, boat launching, tours, and other services and amenities offered at our national parks. Obtain Golden Age and Golden Access Passports in person at any of the attractions where an entrance fee is charged. Be prepared to show proof of age or proof of a medically determined permanent disability to qualify. A onetime $10 processing fee is charged for the Golden Age Passport. Golden Access Passports are free.

ADDITIONAL INFORMATION

- For more information about individual National Park Service properties or to make camping reservations call 1-800-365-2267 or visit *www.nps.gov.*

- Recreation.gov (*www.recreation.gov*) is an easy-to-use Web site with information about all federal recreation areas. The site allows you to search for recreation areas by state, by recreational activity, by agency, or by map.

Take In the Treasures of the Smithsonian Institution

E STABLISHED IN 1846 WITH funds bequeathed to the United States by James Smithson, our "National Museum" is actually comprised of 16 museums and galleries, the National Zoo, and numerous research facilities in the United States and abroad. The reasons why Smithson, a British scientist, left his fortune to the people of the United States to found an institution for the "increase and diffusion of knowledge" remains a mystery.

When most people think of the Smithsonian, they think of Washington, DC, and in fact nine of the Smithsonian's museums are located on the National Mall, between the Washington Monument and the Capitol. Five other museums and the National Zoo also call DC home, while New York City houses the Cooper-Hewitt National Design Museum and the National Museum of the American Indian. The Smithsonian museums currently hold over 140 million artifacts and specimens in their trust.

VISITOR TIPS

- Admission to all Washington, DC, branches of the Smithsonian, including the National Zoo, is free.

- Admission to Cooper-Hewitt National Design Museum in New York requires a fee, although admission to New York's National Museum of the American Indian is free.

- Handheld still and video cameras are permitted in all permanent collection galleries but are prohibited in special exhibitions, and as otherwise posted.

- Flash photography and tripods are not permitted inside the museum buildings unless permission is granted by the museum's Public Affairs Office. Some exceptions apply, so check at the museum information desks.

- The Washington museums are open every day except Christmas from 10 a.m. to 5:30 p.m. Extended summer hours are determined annually so call or visit the Smithsonian Web site for the latest details.

- There is so much to see, you could spend months or even years exploring the Smithsonian collections. The Smithsonian Information Center, located in the Castle at 1000 Jefferson Drive SW, makes a great first stop for your tour, as they can help you plan your time and get the most from your visit. Open daily from 9 a.m. to 5:30 p.m., an hour earlier than the museums, the Information Center can make touring the Smithsonian a little less overwhelming.

- Most museums offer free tours daily on a walk-in basis. For times and other information, check at any museum information desk or go to *www.si.edu/visit*.

- Using public transportation to get to the museums will save you traffic and parking hassles. DC Metrorail stations provide an inexpensive and convenient way to get to most museums and the National Zoo.

- You'll find the museums less crowded right after they open on weekdays.

- Wear comfortable shoes, as you'll do a lot of walking both within the museums and between them.

- The National Museum of American History is closed for renovations through summer 2008.

SECURITY ALERT

Since the Smithsonian museums guard our most important national treasures, security is intense. Be prepared for security officers to check all bags, purses, briefcases, camera bags, or other materials brought in. To expedite the process and create shorter wait times for everyone, the Smithsonian staff reminds visitors:

- Bring only a small purse or "fanny-pack"-style bag.

- Leave backpacks, daypacks, or other large bags in your car or tour bus. For security reasons, most museum lockers and checkrooms have been closed.

- Sharp objects such as knives, screwdrivers, scissors, nail files, and corkscrews are strictly prohibited.

- Bag lunches are not permitted in the museums.

- At the Air and Space, Natural History, and American History Museums all visitors are required to walk through a metal detector and all bags are screened by x-ray machines. Those who are unable to go through the metal detector will be hand-screened with an electronic wand by security personnel.

ADDITIONAL INFORMATION

Smithsonian Information
P.O. Box 37012
SI Building, Room 153, MRC 010
Washington, DC 20013-7012
Voice: (202) 633-1000 or TTY: (202) 633-5285
www.si.edu

Can't visit? Take a virtual tour of the Smithsonian with your computer: *http://2k.si.edu.*

Sing the National Anthem

THE NATIONAL ANTHEM OF the United States of America, written by Francis Scott Key on September 14th, 1814, and designated the national anthem by an Act of Congress in 1931, has four (count them, four) verses. Do you know them all? Neither do most Americans.

It can be an uplifting patriotic experience to attend a public event and join in the singing of this proud song. But believe it or not, some Americans don't even know all the words to the first verse of the song. They may know how to fake it—lip-synching and mumbling during the opening festivities at ball games—but the fact remains that they do not know the words to their own national anthem.

For the purposes of the average public celebration, knowing the first verse of the anthem is plenty to get you by. True patriots, however, will want to know all four verses.

"THE STAR SPANGLED BANNER" BY FRANCIS SCOTT KEY

Oh, say can you see by the dawn's early light
What so proudly we hailed at the twilight's last gleaming?
Whose broad stripes and bright stars through the perilous fight,
O'er the ramparts we watched were so gallantly streaming?

And the rockets' red glare, the bombs bursting in air,
Gave proof through the night that our flag was still there.
Oh, say does that star-spangled banner yet wave
O'er the land of the free, and the home of the brave?

On the shore, dimly seen through the mists of the deep,
Where the foe's haughty host in dread silence reposes,
What is that which the breeze, o'er the towering steep,
As it fitfully blows, half conceals, half discloses?
Now it catches the gleam of the morning's first beam,
In full glory reflected now shines in the stream:
'Tis the star-spangled banner! Oh long may it wave
O'er the land of the free, and the home of the brave!

And where is that band who so vauntingly swore
That the havoc of war and the battle's confusion,
A home and a country, should leave us no more?
Their blood has washed out their foul footsteps' pollution.
No refuge could save the hireling and slave
From the terror of flight, or the gloom of the grave,
And the star-spangled banner in triumph doth wave,
O'er the land of the free, and the home of the brave!

Oh! thus be it ever when freemen shall stand,
Between their loved home, and the war's desolation!
Blest with victory and peace, may the heav'n rescued land
Praise the Power that hath made and preserved us a nation!
Then conquer we must, when our cause it is just,
And this be our motto: "In God is our trust."
And the star-spangled banner in triumph shall wave,
O'er the land of the free, and the home of the brave!

⭐ *Visit the Star-Spangled Banner Flag House*

One of Baltimore's oldest museums, the Star-Spangled Banner Flag House tells the story of Mary Young Pickersgill, the widow who made the enormous 30 by 42 foot flag that flew over Fort McHenry during the War of 1812—the same historic flag that inspired Francis Scott Key to pen his famous poem.

While the actual flag now hangs at the Smithsonian's National Museum of American History, visitors to the Flag House can tour the 1793 home where Mary Pickersgill sewed the banner. The meticulously restored residence offers Americans a glimpse of 1813 Baltimore life as well as an appreciation of the time and labor that went into creating the enormous flag. Also included in a visit to the Flag House is the War of 1812 Museum and a gorgeous garden that includes a unique 17 by 28 foot stone map of the United States. The museum is located at 844 East Pratt Street, Baltimore, Maryland, and is open Tuesday to Saturday, 10 a.m. 4 p.m. and the second Sunday of each month from 10 a.m. to 4 p.m. For more information call (410) 837-1793 or visit *www.flaghouse.org*.

ADDITIONAL INFORMATION

For a biography of Francis Scott Key, visit *www.usflag.org/francis.scott.key.html*.

Top Ten Patriotic Music Selections

NOTHING STIRS THE SOUL like music, and a good patriotic tune can bring tears to the eyes of many a proud American. The scope of favorite patriotic music covers a wide range of styles and moods, from a rousing Sousa march to the deep reflection of "America the Beautiful," and the timeless patriotic sentiments of John Mellencamp's "Our Country." Here are my top ten favorite patriotic musical selections, in no particular order. You'll probably have more of your own to add to the list.

1. **"The Star Spangled Banner"**   Nearly every singer of note has had the honor of singing our national anthem at one time or another, but arguably the most popular version belongs to Whitney Houston. Her classic take on the song, recorded in 1991 at Superbowl XXV, while our country was in the midst of the Persian Gulf War, took the anthem to new heights.

2. **"God Bless America"**   Irving Berlin composed America's unofficial national anthem during the summer of 1918 for his Ziegfeld-style revue, *Yip, Yip, Yaphank*. Ultimately cut from that revue for being too somber, Berlin revised the lyrics and brought the song back in 1938. Kate Smith introduced the new and improved "God Bless America" during her radio broadcast on Armistice Day, 1938, and the song became an immediate smash hit. Berlin soon established the "God Bless America Fund," dedicating the song's royalties to the Boy and Girl Scouts of America. Those looking for some more recent takes on this tune might try recordings by Leann Rimes or Celine Dion.

3. **"God Bless the USA"**   For legions of fans, country superstar Lee Greenwood's patriotic classic, more than any other song, expresses

what it means to be an American. The Country Music Association of America agreed in 1985, when it named "God Bless the USA" song of the year.

4. **"America the Beautiful"** Massachusetts poet Katherine Lee Bates, an English professor at Wellesley College, first published her poem "America the Beautiful" in 1895 after making her first journey to the American west. Eventually the poem was set to music and many great artists have since recorded the song. Check your music stores for fabulous versions by Ray Charles and Elvis Presley.

5. **"Stars and Stripes Forever"** The official march of the United States, John Phillip Sousa's "Stars and Stripes Forever" is undoubtedly his most enduring work. Penned in 1896 while he was en route from Europe to the United States, the march was an immediate success and Sousa's band played it at almost every concert until his death over 25 years later. Sousa even wrote lyrics for his march, although they are rarely ever performed.

6. **"This Land is Your Land"** Recorded for Decca Records on January 7, 1952, during Woody Guthrie's last commercial session, "This Land Is Your Land" has been an American favorite ever since. In fact, Guthrie's original recording is still in print on certain albums. What many people don't realize is that this is actually a protest song, something that becomes apparent when you read all the lyrics, not just the ones commonly heard.

7. **"Yankee Doodle"** While the precise history of the song "Yankee Doodle" remains somewhat murky, the modern version is widely attributed to Richard Shuckburgh, a British Army surgeon who reportedly wrote the song in the early 1750s to ridicule American colonists. It seems that, compared to the prim and proper British

soldiers, the Americans were a shabby, classless group, looked upon as country bumpkins by the British. Despite Shuckburgh's less than honorable intent, American revolutionaries soon adopted the song as their own, and even played it when Cornwallis surrendered at the Battle of Yorktown. Creating new verses as need and imagination dictated—there are said to be as many as 190 verses of "Yankee Doodle"—the colonists didn't hesitate to take creative liberty with Shuckburgh's tune and make it uniquely American.

8. **"You're a Grand Old Flag"** George M. Cohan wrote many patriotic songs, including "Over There" (for which he received a congressional citation), "Yankee Doodle Dandy," and this classic. Originally titled "You're a Grand Old Rag," the name change undoubtedly contributed to the song's lasting popularity.

9. **"Our Country"** I had previously dismissed John Mellencamp's patriotic anthem as nothing more than the soundtrack to a truck commercial. However, Mellencamp's performance of it on Comedy Central's "The Colbert Report" moved me to tears and to the realization that its poignant lyrics represent the ideals of a broad spectrum of patriotic Americans.

10. **"America"** Neil Diamond expressed the hopes and dreams of America's immigrants when he penned this uplifting song for the 1980 movie *The Jazz Singer,* in which he also starred. While the movie was a critical and box office flop, the tune has endured as one of Diamond's most popular.

ADDITIONAL INFORMATION

- The full history of "Yankee Doodle" from *The Straight Dope* is at the site *www.straightdope.com/mailbag/myankeedoodle.html.*

- Lyrics to a host of patriotic songs, including the little known lyrics to "Stars and Stripes Forever," can be found at *www.niehs. nih.gov/kids/musicpatriot.htm*.

- Lyrics to "God Bless the USA" can be found at *www.scoutsongs.com*.

- Lyrics to "Our Country" by John Mellencamp can be found at *www.mellencamp.com*.

- Lyrics to "America" can be found at *www.seeklyrics.com/lyrics/ Neil-Diamond/America.html*.

Display the National Flower

IN 1985 BY SENATE Joint Resolution 159, Congress designated the rose as the National Floral Emblem of the United States of America and authorized and requested the president to issue a proclamation declaring this fact. Ronald Reagan signed Proclamation 557 into effect on November 20, 1986.

For countless reasons, the rose was by far the best bloom for the job, as Reagan so eloquently stated in his proclamation:

Our first President, George Washington, bred roses, and a variety he named after his mother is still grown today. The White House itself boasts a beautiful Rose Garden. We grow roses in all our fifty states. We find roses throughout our art, music, and literature. We decorate our celebrations and parades with roses. Most of all, we present roses to those we love, and we lavish them on our altars, our civil shrines, and the final resting places of our honored dead.

Interestingly enough, the rose is also the national flower of Bulgaria, the Czech Republic, England, Iran, Iraq, Luxembourg, and Turkey.

ADDITIONAL INFORMATION

Tips for growing and displaying your own roses can be found at *www.gardenguides.com/forms/roses.htm.*

Bake an Apple Pie

I T'S OFTEN REPEATED THAT nothing is more American than mom and apple pie. I couldn't agree more, and so will everyone who tastes my all-American mom's best apple pie recipe!

MAKE CRUST

2 cups flour
2 teaspoons salt
²/₃ cup vegetable shortening
3 to 5 tablespoons ice water
1 egg white (for brushing prepared crust)

Measure flour and salt into a large bowl and cut in shortening until mixture is crumbly. Sprinkle in ice water a tablespoon at a time, mixing until all the flour has been moistened. If necessary, add additional water, one tablespoon at a time. Divide dough into two discs, wrap in plastic wrap and chill for at least 15 minutes before rolling.

PREPARE FILLING

*3 ¹/₂ pounds cooking apples (about
  10 medium apples) peeled,
  cored, and thinly sliced*
1 tablespoon lemon juice
*1 tablespoon butter, cut into
  small pieces*
²/₃ cup sugar
2 tablespoons flour
1 ¹/₂ teaspoons cinnamon
¹/₄ teaspoon nutmeg
1 tablespoon sugar

Combine sugar, flour, cinnamon, and nutmeg in a large bowl. Add apples and lemon juice, and toss to combine.

ASSEMBLE PIE AND BAKE

Preheat oven to 425ºF. Roll out bottom piecrust and fit into a 9-inch pie plate. Spoon apple filling into crust and dot with small pieces of butter. Roll out the top crust and cover the apples, sealing the pie with a decorative edge. Cut four or five 1-inch slits in the top crust to allow steam to escape during baking. Brush crust with egg white and sprinkle with 1 tablespoon sugar. Bake for 20 minutes before lowering oven temperature to 375º F. Bake for 1 hour longer or until crust is lightly browned and filling is bubbly. Cool on a wire rack for at least 30 minutes before serving.

- If the crust is getting too brown, cover loosely with aluminum foil during the last 20 minutes of baking.

- The secret to tender, flaky piecrust is to mix and handle the dough as little as possible. Over-handling and over-rolling develops the gluten in the flour and makes the crust tough.

- Keep your oven clean by placing your unbaked pie on a foil-lined cookie sheet to catch any overflow while baking.

ADDITIONAL INFORMATION

- Piecrust *Tutorial—www.fabulousfoods.com/school/cstech/piecrusts. html*

- Video Instructions for Rolling Piecrusts—*www.taunton.com/ finecooking/pages/cvt006.asp*

- More Apple Information and Recipes—The Washington Apple Web site offers a wealth of information and tasty recipes at *www.bestapples.com*

☆ *Johnny Appleseed*

A colorful character of the 1800s Indiana frontier, John Chapman, aka "Johnny Appleseed" roamed the American wilderness on foot planting apple trees and creating orchards in Pennsylvania, Ohio, Kentucky, Illinois, and Indiana. He covered an estimated area of 100,000 square miles, and some of Chapman's original trees still bear fruit today.

The exact reason for John Chapman's unusual quest remains a mystery, although it's rumored he dreamed of a land where no one went hungry because apples were plentiful. Even during his lifetime, John's gentleness and kindness were as legendary as his eccentricities. He walked through the wilderness alone and without weapons. He gained the respect and admiration of both the Native American tribes and the new settlers. He lived simply, slept outdoors, walked barefoot even in winter, and maintained a vegetarian diet. Garbed in old and shabby clothes—he sometimes even dressed in a potato sack with holes cut out for his arms and legs and wore a tin kettle for a hat—he spread his message of peace and good will.

It wasn't discovered until after his death in 1845 that John Chapman was not a pauper. In spite of his humble lifestyle, he owned (and leased) vast areas of land—land abundantly populated with apple trees, of course. Johnny Appleseed is buried in Fort Wayne, Indiana, at Archer Park, where each year they celebrate the spirit of this American folk hero at the annual Johnny Appleseed Festival. For more information, contact the Johnny Appleseed Festival, 1502 Harry Baals Drive, Fort Wayne IN 46805; (219) 427-6003; *www.johnnyappleseedfest.com*.

Appendix A

Flag Etiquette

SINCE THE TRAGIC EVENTS of September 11, 2001, Americans are proudly flying "Old Glory" like never before. Unfortunately, in their enthusiasm to show patriotic unity, many people are unknowingly ignoring proper rules and etiquette of when and how to display the flag. Follow these guidelines, excerpted from the National Flag Code, and you'll always display your flag with dignity and pride, no matter what the occasion.

- It is the universal custom to display the flag only from sunrise to sunset on buildings and on stationary flagstaffs in the open. However, the flag may be displayed twenty-four hours a day if properly illuminated during the hours of darkness.

- Flags displayed in inclement weather need to be of an all-weather variety designed to withstand the elements.

- The flag should be hoisted briskly and lowered ceremoniously.

- To display the flag from a building, hang it on a staff or rope with the stars away from the building.

- When marching, carry the flag on the right in a procession or parade. If there are many other flags, carry the American flag in the front center position.

- No other flag or pennant should be placed above or, if on the same level, to the right of the flag of the United States of America.

- When flags of states, cities, or societies are flown on the same halyard with the Stars and Stripes, the American flag should always be at the peak.

- When the flags of two or more nations are displayed, they are to be flown from separate staffs of the same height. The flags should be of approximately equal size. International usage forbids the display of the flag of one nation above that of another nation in times of peace.

- The U.S. flag should always be on its own right in relation to other flags on adjacent staffs—to the left of the observer.

- On a car, attach the flag to the antenna or clamp the flagstaff to the right fender of a vehicle, but never lay the flag over the vehicle.

- When displayed either horizontally or vertically against a wall or in a window, the stars should be uppermost and to the observer's left.

- When carrying the flag, hold it at a slight angle from your body. It is also proper to carry the flag with one hand and rest it on your right shoulder.

- At a funeral, drape the flag over the casket with the stars at the head and over the left shoulder of the body. Do not lower the flag into the grave or allow it to touch the ground.

Half-Staff Rules

- By order of the president, the flag shall be flown at half-staff upon the death of principal figures of the United States government or the governor of a state, territory, or possession, as a mark of respect to their memory. In the event of the death of other officials or foreign dignitaries, the flag is to be displayed at half-staff according to presidential instructions or orders, or in accordance with recognized customs or practices not inconsistent with law.

- When flown at half-staff, the flag should be first hoisted to the peak for an instant and then lowered to the half-staff position. The flag should be again raised to the peak before it is lowered for the day.

- On Memorial Day, the flag should be displayed at half-staff until noon only, then raised to the top of the staff.

FLAG DON'TS

- The United States Flag Code provides many rules for how, when, and why the flag may be displayed, but it also warns of some important flag don'ts to avoid:

- The flag should not be displayed on a float in a parade, except from a staff, and should not be draped over the hood, top, sides, or back of any vehicle, railroad train, or boat.

- While it's permissible for the flag to form a distinctive feature of the unveiling ceremony of a statue or monument, it should never be used as the actual covering piece.

- When it is permissible to use the flag to cover a casket, it should never be lowered into the grave or allowed to touch the ground.

- When being carried, the flag should not be dipped to any person or thing. Regimental colors, state flags, and organization or institutional flags are to be dipped to the American flag as a mark of honor.

- The flag should never be displayed with the union down, except as a signal of dire distress in instances of extreme danger to life or property.

- The flag should never touch anything beneath it, such as the ground, water, or merchandise.

- The flag should never be carried flat or horizontally, but always aloft and free.

- The flag should never be used as wearing apparel, bedding, or drapery. It should never be festooned, drawn back, nor up, in folds, but always allowed to fall free. Bunting of blue, white, and red, always arranged with the blue above, the white in the middle, and the red below, should be used for covering a speaker's desk, draping the front of the platform, and for general decoration.

- The flag should never be fastened, displayed, used, or stored in such a manner as to permit it to be easily torn, soiled, or damaged in any way.

- The flag should never be used as a covering for a ceiling.

- The flag should never have placed upon it, nor on any part of it, nor attached to it, any mark, insignia, letter, word, figure, design, picture, or drawing of any nature.

- The flag should never be used as a receptacle for receiving, holding, carrying, or delivering anything.

- The flag should never be used for advertising purposes in any manner whatsoever. It should not be embroidered on such articles as cushions or handkerchiefs and the like, printed or otherwise impressed on paper napkins or boxes or anything that is designed for temporary use and discard. Advertising signs should not be fastened to a staff or halyard from which the flag is flown.

- No part of the flag should ever be used as a costume or athletic uniform. However, a flag patch may be affixed to the uniform of military personnel, firefighters, police officers, and members of patriotic organizations. The flag represents a living country and is itself considered a living thing. Therefore, the lapel flag pin being a replica, should be worn on the left lapel near the heart.

HISTORY AND SYMBOLISM OF
THE UNITED STATES FLAG

Before there was a Stars and Stripes, there was a Grand Union Flag—the first flag of the colonists that had any resemblance to our present emblem. Alike were the 13 alternating red and white stripes, representing the original 13 colonies: however, the red cross of St. George of England superimposed over the white cross of St. Andrew of Scotland adorned the Grand Union Flag's field of blue, not stars.

The banner remained our unofficial national flag and ensign of the navy until June 14, 1777, when the Marine Committee of the Second Continental Congress at Philadelphia authorized the Stars and Stripes and put the matter to rest:

Resolved, that the flag of the United States be thirteen stripes, alternate red and white; that the union be thirteen stars, white in a blue field representing a new constellation.

Since the resolution gave no specific instructions as to how many points the stars should have, or where they should be arranged on the blue union, you'll find all kinds of creative variations when looking at historic flags in museums. Some flag-maker's flags staggered their stars in rows, others made circles of the 13 stars while still others opted for completely random placement. Some stars had six points while others sported eight and the proportional ratio of the blue field to stripes varied from flag to flag. The matter was never completely solved until the signing of the Executive Order of June 24, 1912, which regulated such aesthetic matters.

Contrary to popular belief, there is no actual proof, but only anecdotal evidence, that Betsy Ross made the very first Stars and Stripes flag. It is known that Betsy did make many flags over a period of about 50 years, including many for the Pennsylvania State Navy. The legend first came to pass when William J. Canby, a grandson of Betsy's, before a meeting of the Historical Society of Pennsylvania in 1870, first publicly told the story he had heard as a young child from his grandmother. Canby claimed that Colonel Ross, with Robert Morris and General Washington, commissioned his grandmother to make a flag from a rough drawing they brought to her. Canby speculated the date to be June of 1776, prior to the signing of the Declaration of Independence.

★ Flag Day

June 14 is the flag's official birthday and each year Americans throughout the country celebrate in Flag Day ceremonies on this day. The Stars and Stripes first flew in Flag Day festivities in 1861 in Hartford, Connecticut, and the first national observance of Flag Day took place on the 100 year anniversary of the flag, June 14, 1877.

President Woodrow Wilson made Flag Day official in 1916, but it took Congress and President Harry Truman until 1949 to make this day a permanent observance. Although it is not celebrated as a federal holiday, Americans everywhere continue to honor the flag and the ideals it represents to them through school programs and civic observances on June 14.

PROPERLY SALUTE THE FLAG

Believe it or not, the clothing you wear affects how to properly salute the flag. Civilians should place their right hands over their hearts, except when wearing athletic clothing, in which case they should remove their hats and stand at attention. No hand salute is necessary. Civilian men wearing hats should remove the hat and hold it at their left shoulder, with hand over heart. Aliens should simply stand at attention. Of course, those in uniform should render the military salute.

When the flag is moving, as in a parade, it is proper to salute when it is six paces in front of you and hold the salute until it passes six paces beyond. During the playing of the national anthem, the salute to the flag begins with the first note and continues until the song has ended. Even when a flag is not on display during the playing of the anthem, it is still proper to face the music and salute as if it were actually there.

THE PLEDGE OF ALLEGIANCE

The pledge was originally penned for a public school program celebrating the 400th anniversary of Columbus's discovery of America. Originally published anonymously in the September 8 issue of *The Youth's Companion,* a leading family periodical of its day, authorship is generally credited to Francis Bellamy, who worked at the magazine.

The pledge wasn't always said with the right hand over the heart, but rather in the so-called "Bellamy Salute"—hand resting outward from the chest, then the arm extending out from the body. After Adolph Hitler came to power in Europe, many Americans became concerned that the Bellamy salute too closely resembled the Nazi military salute, so Congress established the current practice of reciting the pledge with the right hand over the heart in 1942.

More than 12 million children recited the Pledge of Allegiance on the historic Columbus Day of 1892, just like children all over the country still recite the pledge today . . . well, almost. The language has slightly evolved over the years.

The Original Pledge of Allegiance

> *I pledge allegiance to my Flag and*
> *to the Republic for which it stands:*
> *one Nation indivisible, with Liberty*
> *and Justice for all.*

The words "the flag of the United States" replaced "my flag" in 1923. A year later, the words "of America" were added after "United States." The new wording took away the possibility of foreign-born people saluting the flag of their birth country instead of the United States flag. The final change in the pledge's language came on Flag Day 1954, when Congress passed the law that added the words "under God" after "one nation."

The Current Pledge of Allegiance

I pledge allegiance to the flag of the United States of America and to the Republic for which it stands, one Nation under God, indivisible, with liberty and justice for all.

The pledge, in any of its variations, never received formal recognition from Congress until it was officially adopted into the U.S. Flag Code on Flag Day of 1942; however, the official name "The Pledge of Allegiance" wasn't adopted until 1945. It took only one year after recognizing the pledge for the Supreme Court to rule that school children could not be forced to recite it.

PROPERLY FOLD AND STORE THE FLAG

According to the United States Flag Code, when the flag is lowered, no part of it should touch the ground or any other object; it should be received by waiting hands and arms. The flag should also be cleaned and mended whenever necessary.

Folding the Flag

A properly folded flag ends up in the shape of a tri-cornered hat, symbolic of the hats worn by colonial soldiers during the Revolutionary War.

1. Start by holding the flag waist-high with another person so that its surface is parallel to the ground.

2. Fold the flag in half, lengthwise, bringing the lower striped section up to meet the upper field of blue.

3. Fold lengthwise again, keeping the blue field on the outside.

4. Make a triangular fold by bringing the striped corner of the folded edge to meet the top (open) edge of the flag.

5. Fold the outermost point on the right inward, parallel to the top open edge, which forms a second triangle.

6. Continue the triangular folding until the entire length of the flag is folded in this manner. When complete, only a triangular blue field of stars should be visible.

Burning the Flag

When a flag is so worn it is no longer fit to serve as a symbol of our country, it should be destroyed by burning it in a dignified manner. Check with your local American Legion post before Flag Day, as most posts conduct flag burning ceremonies on June 14.

ADDITIONAL INFORMATION

- The Boy Scouts of America share three flag burning ceremonies for proper retirement of worn flags at *www.usscouts.org/usscouts/ceremony/flagret2.html.*

- For everything you've ever wanted to know about the flag (and then some), go to *www.usflag.org.* The site includes a full copy of the U.S. Flag Code at *www.usflag.org/uscode36.html.*

Appendix B

The Declaration of Independence

THE UNANIMOUS DECLARATION OF the thirteen united States of America. When in the Course of human events, it becomes necessary for one people to dissolve the political bands which have connected them with another, and to assume among the Powers of the earth, the separate and equal station to which the Laws of Nature and of Nature's God entitle them, a decent respect to the opinions of mankind requires that they should declare the causes which impel them to the separation.

We hold these truths to be self-evident, that all men are created equal, that they are endowed by their Creator with certain unalienable Rights, that among these are Life, Liberty, and the pursuit of Happiness. That to secure these rights, Governments are instituted among Men, deriving their just powers from the consent of the governed, That whenever any Form of Government becomes destructive of these ends, it is the Right of the People to alter or to abolish it, and to institute new Government, laying its foundation on such principles and organizing its powers in such form, as to them shall seem most likely to effect their Safety and Happiness. Prudence, indeed, will dictate that Governments long established should not be changed for light and transient causes; and accordingly all experience hath shewn, that mankind are more disposed to suffer, while evils are sufferable, than to right themselves by abolishing the forms to which they are accustomed. But when a long train of abuses and usurpations, pursuing invariably the same Object evinces a design to reduce them under absolute Despotism, it is their right, it is their duty, to throw off such Government, and to provide new Guards for their future security. Such has been the patient sufferance of these Colonies; and such is now the necessity which constrains them to alter their former Systems of Government. The history of the present King of Great Britain is a history of repeated injuries and usurpations, all having in direct object the establishment of an absolute Tyranny over these States. To prove this, let Facts be submitted to a candid world.

He has refused his Assent to Laws, the most wholesome and necessary for the public good.

He has forbidden his Governors to pass Laws of immediate and pressing importance, unless suspended in their operation till his Assent should be obtained; and when so suspended, he has utterly neglected to attend to them.

He has refused to pass other Laws for the accommodation of large districts of people, unless those people would relinquish the right of Representation in the Legislature, a right inestimable to them and formidable to tyrants only.

He has called together legislative bodies at places unusual, uncomfortable, and distant from the depository of their public Records, for the sole purpose of fatiguing them into compliance with his measures.

He has dissolved Representative Houses repeatedly, for opposing with manly firmness his invasions on the rights of the people.

He has refused for a long time, after such dissolutions, to cause others to be elected; whereby the Legislative Powers, incapable of Annihilation, have returned to the People at large for their exercise; the State remaining in the mean time exposed to all the dangers of invasion from without, and convulsions within.

He has endeavoured to prevent the population of these States; for that purpose obstructing the Laws for Naturalization of

Foreigners; refusing to pass others to encourage their migrations hither, and raising the conditions of new Appropriations of Lands.

He has obstructed the Administration of Justice, by refusing his Assent to Laws for establishing Judiciary Powers.

He has made Judges dependent on his Will alone, for the tenure of their offices, and the amount and payment of their salaries.

He has erected a multitude of New Offices, and sent hither swarms of Officers to harrass our people, and eat out their substance.

He has kept among us, in times of peace, Standing Armies without the Consent of our legislature.

He has affected to render the Military independent of and superior to the Civil power.

He has combined with others to subject us to a jurisdiction foreign to our constitution, and unacknowledged by our laws; giving his Assent to their Acts of pretended legislation:

For quartering large bodies of armed troops among us:

For protecting them, by a mock Trial, from punishment for any Murders which they should commit on the Inhabitants of these States:

For cutting off our Trade with all parts of the world:

For imposing taxes on us without our Consent:

For depriving us in many cases, of the benefits of Trial by Jury:

For transporting us beyond Seas to be tried for pretended offences:

For abolishing the free System of English Laws in a neighbouring Province, establishing therein an Arbitrary government, and enlarging its Boundaries so as to render it at once an example and fit instrument for introducing the same absolute rule into these Colonies:

For taking away our Charters, abolishing our most valuable Laws, and altering fundamentally the Forms of our Governments:

For suspending our own Legislatures, and declaring themselves invested with Power to legislate for us in all cases whatsoever.

He has abdicated Government here, by declaring us out of his Protection and waging War against us.

He has plundered our seas, ravaged our Coasts, burnt our towns, and destroyed the lives of our people.

He is at this time transporting large armies of foreign mercenaries to compleat the works of death, desolation and tyranny, already begun with circumstances of Cruelty & perfidy scarcely paralleled in the most barbarous ages, and totally unworthy the Head of a civilized nation.

He has constrained our fellow Citizens taken Captive on the high Seas to bear Arms against their Country, to become the executioners of their friends and Brethren, or to fall themselves by their Hands.

He has excited domestic insurrections amongst us, and has endeavoured to bring on the inhabitants of our frontiers, the merciless Indian Savages, whose known rule of warfare is an undistinguished destruction of all ages, sexes and conditions.

In every stage of these Oppressions We have Petitioned for Redress in the most humble terms: Our repeated Petitions have been answered only by repeated injury. A Prince, whose character is thus marked by every act which may define a Tyrant, is unfit to be the ruler of a free People.

Nor have We been wanting in attentions to our Brittish brethren. We have warned them from time to time of attempts by their legislature to extend an unwarrantable jurisdiction over us. We have reminded them of the circumstances of our emigration and settlement here. We have appealed to their native justice and magnanimity, and we have conjured them by the ties of our common kindred to disavow these usurpations, which, would inevitably interrupt our connections and correspondence. They too have been deaf to the voice of justice and of consanguinity. We must, therefore, acquiesce in the necessity, which denounces our Separation, and hold them, as we hold the rest of mankind, Enemies in War, in Peace Friends.

We, therefore, the Representatives of the United States of America, in General Congress, Assembled, appealing to the Supreme Judge of the world for the rectitude of our intentions, do, in the Name, and by Authority of the good People of these Colonies, solemnly publish and declare, That these United Colonies are, and of Right ought to be Free and Independent States; that they are Absolved from all Allegiance to the British Crown, and that all political connection between them and the State of Great Britain, is and ought to be totally dissolved; and that as Free and Independent States, they have full Power to levy War, conclude Peace, contract Alliances, establish Commerce, and to do all other Acts and Things which Independent States may of right do. And for the support of this Declaration, with a firm reliance on the Protection of Divine Providence, we mutually pledge to each other our Lives, our Fortunes and our sacred Honor.

 ## The 56 Signatures of the Declaration of Independence

- **Connecticut**: Roger Sherman, Samuel Huntington, William Williams, Oliver Wolcott

- **Delaware**: Caesar Rodney, George Read, Thomas McKean

- **Georgia**: Button Gwinnett, Lyman Hall, George Walton

- **Maryland**: Samuel Chase, William Paca, Thomas Stone, Charles Carroll of Carrollton

- **Massachusetts**: John Hancock, Samuel Adams, John Adams, Robert Treat Paine, Elbridge Gerry

- **New Hampshire:** Josiah Bartlett, William Whipple, Matthew Thornton

- **New Jersey**: Richard Stockton, John Witherspoon, Francis Hopkinson, John Hart, Abraham Clark

- **New York**: William Floyd, Philip Livingston, Francis Lewis, Lewis Morris

- **North Carolina:** William Hooper, Joseph Hewes, John Penn

- **Pennsylvania**: Robert Morris, Benjamin Rush, Benjamin Franklin, John Morton, George Clymer, James Smith, George Taylor, James Wilson, George Ross

- **Rhode Island**: Stephen Hopkins, William Ellery

- **South Carolina**: Edward Rutledge, Thomas Heyward, Jr., Thomas Lynch, Jr., Arthur Middleton

- **Virginia**: George Wythe, Richard Henry Lee, Thomas Jefferson, Benjamin Harrison, Thomas Nelson, Jr., Francis Lightfoot Lee, Carter Braxton

---

☆ *TV Trivia*

Martin Sheen's character on television's *The West Wing* series, President Josiah Bartlett, was named for one of the original signers of the Declaration of Independence. Both the actual and fictional Bartlett hailed from New Hampshire.

THE FOLLOWING TEXT IS a transcription of the Constitution in its original form. Items in *italics* have since been amended or superseded.

THE CONSTITUTION OF THE UNITED STATES OF AMERICA

We the People of the United States, in Order to form a more perfect Union, establish Justice, insure domestic Tranquility, provide for the common defense, promote the general Welfare, and secure the Blessings of Liberty to ourselves and our Posterity, do ordain and establish this Constitution for the United States of America.

Article. I.

SECTION. 1.

All legislative Powers herein granted shall be vested in a Congress of the United States, which shall consist of a Senate and House of Representatives.

SECTION. 2.

The House of Representatives shall be composed of Members chosen every second Year by the People of the several States, and the Electors in each State shall have the Qualifications requisite for Electors of the most numerous Branch of the State Legislature.

No Person shall be a Representative who shall not have attained to the Age of twenty five Years, and been seven Years a Citizen of the United States, and who shall not, when elected, be an Inhabitant of that State in which he shall be chosen.

Representatives and direct Taxes shall be apportioned among the several States which may be included within this Union, according to their respective Numbers, which shall be determined by adding to the whole

Number of free Persons, including those bound to Service for a Term of Years, and excluding Indians not taxed, three fifths of all other Persons. The actual Enumeration shall be made within three Years after the first Meeting of the Congress of the United States, and within every subsequent Term of ten Years, in such Manner as they shall by Law direct. The Number of Representatives shall not exceed one for every thirty Thousand, but each State shall have at Least one Representative; and until such enumeration shall be made, the State of New Hampshire shall be entitled to chuse three, Massachusetts eight, Rhode-Island and Providence Plantations one, Connecticut five, New-York six, New Jersey four, Pennsylvania eight, Delaware one, Maryland six, Virginia ten, North Carolina five, South Carolina five, and Georgia three.

When vacancies happen in the Representation from any State, the Executive Authority thereof shall issue Writs of Election to fill such Vacancies.

The House of Representatives shall chuse their Speaker and other Officers; and shall have the sole Power of Impeachment.

SECTION. 3.

The Senate of the United States shall be composed of two Senators from each State, *chosen by the Legislature thereof* for six Years; and each Senator shall have one Vote.

Immediately after they shall be assembled in Consequence of the first Election, they shall be divided as equally as may be into three Classes. The Seats of the Senators of the first Class shall be vacated at the Expiration of the second Year, of the second Class at the Expiration of the fourth Year, and of the third Class at the Expiration of the sixth Year, so that one third may be chosen every second Year; *and if Vacancies happen by Resignation, or otherwise, during the Recess of the Legislature of any State, the Executive thereof may make temporary Appointments until the next Meeting of the Legislature, which shall then fill such Vacancies.*

No Person shall be a Senator who shall not have attained to the Age of thirty Years, and been nine Years a Citizen of the United States, and who shall not, when elected, be an Inhabitant of that State for which he shall be chosen.

The Vice President of the United States shall be President of the Senate, but shall have no Vote, unless they be equally divided.

The Senate shall chuse their other Officers, and also a President pro tempore, in the Absence of the Vice President, or when he shall exercise the Office of President of the United States.

The Senate shall have the sole Power to try all Impeachments. When sitting for that Purpose, they shall be on Oath or Affirmation. When the President of the United States is tried, the Chief Justice shall preside: And no Person shall be convicted without the Concurrence of two thirds of the Members present.

Judgment in Cases of Impeachment shall not extend further than to removal from Office, and disqualification to hold and enjoy any Office of honor, Trust or Profit under the United States: but the Party convicted shall nevertheless be liable and subject to Indictment, Trial, Judgment and Punishment, according to Law.

SECTION. 4.

The Times, Places and Manner of holding Elections for Senators and Representatives, shall be prescribed in each State by the Legislature thereof; but the Congress may at any time by Law make or alter such Regulations, except as to the Places of chusing Senators.

The Congress shall assemble at least once in every Year, and such Meeting *shall be on the first Monday in December,* unless they shall by Law appoint a different Day.

SECTION. 5.

Each House shall be the Judge of the Elections, Returns and Qualifications of its own Members, and a Majority of each shall constitute a Quorum to do Business; but a smaller Number may adjourn from day to day, and may be authorized to compel the Attendance of absent Members, in such Manner, and under such Penalties as each House may provide.

Each House may determine the Rules of its Proceedings, punish its Members for disorderly Behaviour, and, with the Concurrence of two thirds, expel a Member.

Each House shall keep a Journal of its Proceedings, and from time to time publish the same, excepting such Parts as may in their Judgment require Secrecy; and the Yeas and Nays of the Members of either House on any question shall, at the Desire of one fifth of those Present, be entered on the Journal.

Neither House, during the Session of Congress, shall, without the Consent of the other, adjourn for more than three days, nor to any other Place than that in which the two Houses shall be sitting.

SECTION. 6.

The Senators and Representatives shall receive a Compensation for their Services, to be ascertained by Law, and paid out of the Treasury of the United States. They shall in all Cases, except Treason, Felony and Breach of the Peace, be privileged from Arrest during their Attendance at the Session of their respective Houses, and in going to and returning from the same; and for any Speech or Debate in either House, they shall not be questioned in any other Place.

No Senator or Representative shall, during the Time for which he was elected, be appointed to any civil Office under the Authority of the United States, which shall have been created, or the Emoluments whereof shall have been increased during such time; and no Person holding any Office under the United States, shall be a Member of either House during his Continuance in Office.

SECTION. 7.

All Bills for raising Revenue shall originate in the House of

Representatives; but the Senate may propose or concur with Amendments as on other Bills.

Every Bill which shall have passed the House of Representatives and the Senate, shall, before it become a Law, be presented to the President of the United States: If he approve he shall sign it, but if not he shall return it, with his Objections to that House in which it shall have originated, who shall enter the Objections at large on their Journal, and proceed to reconsider it. If after such Reconsideration two thirds of that House shall agree to pass the Bill, it shall be sent, together with the Objections, to the other House, by which it shall likewise be reconsidered, and if approved by two thirds of that House, it shall become a Law. But in all such Cases the Votes of both Houses shall be determined by Yeas and Nays, and the Names of the Persons voting for and against the Bill shall be entered on the Journal of each House respectively. If any Bill shall not be returned by the President within ten Days (Sundays excepted) after it shall have been presented to him, the Same shall be a Law, in like Manner as if he had signed it, unless the Congress by their Adjournment prevent its Return, in which Case it shall not be a Law.

Every Order, Resolution, or Vote to which the Concurrence of the Senate and House of Representatives may be necessary (except on a question of Adjournment) shall be presented to the President of the United States; and before the Same shall take Effect, shall be approved by him, or being disapproved by him, shall be repassed by two thirds of the Senate and House of Representatives, according to the Rules and Limitations prescribed in the Case of a Bill.

SECTION. 8.

The Congress shall have Power To lay and collect Taxes, Duties, Imposts and Excises, to pay the Debts and provide for the common Defence and general Welfare of the United States; but all Duties,

Imposts and Excises shall be uniform throughout the United States;

To borrow Money on the credit of the United States;

To regulate Commerce with foreign Nations, and among the several States, and with the Indian Tribes;

To establish an uniform Rule of Naturalization, and uniform Laws on the subject of Bankruptcies throughout the United States;

To coin Money, regulate the Value thereof, and of foreign Coin, and fix the Standard of Weights and Measures;

To provide for the Punishment of counterfeiting the Securities and current Coin of the United States;

To establish Post Offices and post Roads;

To promote the Progress of Science and useful Arts, by securing for limited Times to Authors and Inventors the exclusive Right to their respective Writings and Discoveries;

To constitute Tribunals inferior to the supreme Court;

To define and punish Piracies and Felonies committed on the high Seas, and Offences against the Law of Nations;

To declare War, grant Letters of Marque and Reprisal, and make Rules concerning Captures on Land and Water;

To raise and support Armies, but no Appropriation of Money to that Use shall be for a longer Term than two Years;

To provide and maintain a Navy;

To make Rules for the Government and Regulation of the land and naval Forces;

To provide for calling forth the Militia to execute the Laws of the Union, suppress Insurrections and repel Invasions;

To provide for organizing, arming, and disciplining, the Militia, and for governing such Part of them as may be employed in the Service of the United States, reserving to the States respectively, the Appointment of the Officers, and the Authority of training the Militia according to the discipline prescribed by Congress;

To exercise exclusive Legislation in all Cases whatsoever, over such District (not exceeding ten Miles square) as may, by Cession of particular States, and the Acceptance of Congress, become the Seat of the Government of the United States, and to exercise like Authority over all Places purchased by the Consent of the Legislature of the State in which the Same shall be, for the Erection of Forts, Magazines, Arsenals, dock-Yards, and other needful Buildings;— And

To make all Laws which shall be necessary and proper for carrying into Execution the foregoing Powers, and all other Powers vested by this Constitution in the Government of the United States, or in any Department or Officer thereof.

SECTION. 9.

The Migration or Importation of such Persons as any of the States now existing shall think proper to admit, shall not be prohibited by the Congress prior to the Year one thousand eight hundred and eight, but a Tax or duty may be imposed on such Importation, not exceeding ten dollars for each Person.

The Privilege of the Writ of Habeas Corpus shall not be suspended, unless when in Cases of Rebellion or Invasion the public Safety may require it.

No Bill of Attainder or ex post facto Law shall be passed.

No Capitation, or other direct, Tax shall be laid, *unless in Proportion to the Census or enumeration herein before directed to be taken.*

No Tax or Duty shall be laid on Articles exported from any State.

No Preference shall be given by any Regulation of Commerce or Revenue to the Ports of one State over those of another; nor shall Vessels bound to, or from, one State, be obliged to enter, clear, or pay Duties in another.

No Money shall be drawn from the Treasury, but in Consequence of Appropriations made by Law; and a regular Statement and Account of the Receipts and Expenditures of all public Money shall be published from time to time.

No Title of Nobility shall be granted by the United States: And no Person holding any Office of Profit or Trust under them, shall, without the Consent of the Congress, accept of any present, Emolument, Office, or Title, of any kind whatever, from any King, Prince, or foreign State.

SECTION. 10.

No State shall enter into any Treaty, Alliance, or Confederation; grant Letters of Marque and Reprisal; coin Money; emit Bills of Credit; make any Thing but gold and silver Coin a Tender in Payment of Debts; pass any Bill of Attainder, ex post facto Law, or Law impairing the Obligation of Contracts, or grant any Title of Nobility.

No State shall, without the Consent of the Congress, lay any Imposts or Duties on Imports or Exports, except what may be absolutely necessary for executing its inspection Laws: and the net Produce of all Duties and Imposts, laid by any State on Imports or Exports, shall be for the Use of the Treasury of the United States; and all such Laws shall be subject to the Revision and Controul of the Congress.

No State shall, without the Consent of Congress, lay any Duty of Tonnage, keep Troops, or Ships of War in time of Peace, enter into any Agreement or Compact with another State, or with a foreign Power, or engage in War, unless actually invaded, or in such imminent Danger as will not admit of delay.

Article. II.

SECTION. 1.

The executive Power shall be vested in a President of the United States of America. He shall hold his Office during the Term of four Years, and, together with the Vice President, chosen for the same Term, be elected, as follows:

Each State shall appoint, in such Manner as the Legislature

thereof may direct, a Number of Electors, equal to the whole Number of Senators and Representatives to which the State may be entitled in the Congress: but no Senator or Representative, or Person holding an Office of Trust or Profit under the United States, shall be appointed an Elector.

The Electors shall meet in their respective States, and vote by Ballot for two Persons, of whom one at least shall not be an Inhabitant of the same State with themselves. And they shall make a List of all the Persons voted for, and of the Number of Votes for each; which List they shall sign and certify, and transmit sealed to the Seat of the Government of the United States, directed to the President of the Senate. The President of the Senate shall, in the Presence of the Senate and House of Representatives, open all the Certificates, and the Votes shall then be counted. The Person having the greatest Number of Votes shall be the President, if such Number be a Majority of the whole Number of Electors appointed; and if there be more than one who have such Majority, and have an equal Number of Votes, then the House of Representatives shall immediately chuse by Ballot one of them for President; and if no Person have a Majority, then from the five highest on the List the said House shall in like Manner chuse the President. But in chusing the President, the Votes shall be taken by States, the Representation from each State having one Vote; A quorum for this purpose shall consist of a Member or Members from two thirds of the States, and a Majority of all the States shall be necessary to a Choice. In every Case, after the Choice of the President, the Person having the greatest Number of Votes of the Electors shall be the Vice President. But if there should remain two or more who have equal Votes, the Senate shall chuse from them by Ballot the Vice President.

The Congress may determine the Time of chusing the Electors, and the Day on which they shall give their Votes; which Day shall be the same throughout the United States.

No Person except a natural born Citizen, or a Citizen of the United States, at the time of the Adoption of this Constitution, shall be eligible to the Office of President; neither shall any Person be eligible to that Office who shall not have attained to the Age of thirty five Years, and been fourteen Years a Resident within the United States.

In Case of the Removal of the President from Office, or of his Death, Resignation, or Inability to discharge the Powers and Duties of the said Office, the Same shall devolve on the Vice President, and the Congress may by Law provide for the Case of Removal, Death, Resignation or Inability, both of the President and Vice President, declaring what Officer shall then act as President, and such Officer shall act accordingly, until the Disability be removed, or a President shall be elected.

The President shall, at stated Times, receive for his Services, a Compensation, which shall neither be increased nor diminished during the Period for which he shall have been elected, and he shall not receive within that Period any other Emolument from the United States, or any of them.

Before he enter on the Execution of his Office, he shall take the following Oath or Affirmation:—"I do solemnly swear (or affirm) that I will faithfully execute the Office of President of the United States, and will to the best of my Ability, preserve, protect and defend the Constitution of the United States."

SECTION. 2.

The President shall be Commander in Chief of the Army and Navy of the United States, and of the Militia of the several States, when called into the actual Service of the United States; he may require the Opinion, in writing, of the principal Officer in each of the executive Departments, upon any Subject relating to the Duties of their respective Offices, and he shall have Power to grant Reprieves and Pardons for Offences against the United States, except in Cases of Impeachment.

He shall have Power, by and with the Advice and Consent of the Senate, to make Treaties, provided two thirds of the Senators present concur; and he shall nominate, and by and with the Advice and Consent of the Senate, shall appoint Ambassadors, other public Ministers and Consuls, Judges of the supreme Court, and all other Officers of the United States, whose Appointments are not herein otherwise provided for, and which shall be established by Law: but the Congress may by Law vest the Appointment of such inferior Officers, as they think proper, in the President alone, in the Courts of Law, or in the Heads of Departments.

The President shall have Power to fill up all Vacancies that may happen during the Recess of the Senate, by granting Commissions which shall expire at the End of their next Session.

SECTION. 3.

He shall from time to time give to the Congress Information of the State of the Union, and recommend to their Consideration such Measures as he shall judge necessary and expedient; he may, on extraordinary Occasions, convene both Houses, or either of them, and in Case of Disagreement between them, with Respect to the Time of Adjournment, he may adjourn them to such Time as he shall think proper; he shall receive Ambassadors and other public Ministers; he shall take Care that the Laws be faithfully executed, and shall Commission all the Officers of the United States.

SECTION. 4.

The President, Vice President and all civil Officers of the United States, shall be removed from Office on Impeachment for, and Conviction of, Treason, Bribery, or other high Crimes and Misdemeanors.

Article. III.
SECTION. 1.

The judicial Power of the United States shall be vested in one supreme Court, and in such inferior Courts as the Congress may from time to time ordain and establish. The Judges, both of the supreme and inferior Courts, shall hold their Offices during good Behaviour, and shall, at stated Times, receive for their Services a Compensation, which shall not be diminished during their Continuance in Office.

SECTION. 2.

The judicial Power shall extend to all Cases, in Law and Equity, arising under this Constitution, the Laws of the United States, and Treaties made, or which shall be made, under their Authority;—to all Cases affecting Ambassadors, other public Ministers and Consuls;—to all Cases of admiralty and maritime Jurisdiction;—to Controversies to which the United States shall be a Party;—to Controversies between two or more States;—*between a State and Citizens of another State*;—between Citizens of different States;—between Citizens of the same State claiming Lands under Grants of different States, and between a State, or the Citizens thereof, and foreign States, Citizens or Subjects.

In all Cases affecting Ambassadors, other public Ministers and Consuls, and those in which a State shall be Party, the supreme Court shall have original Jurisdiction. In all the other Cases before mentioned, the supreme Court shall have appellate Jurisdiction, both as to Law and Fact, with such Exceptions, and under such Regulations as the Congress shall make.

The Trial of all Crimes, except in Cases of Impeachment, shall be by Jury; and such Trial shall be held in the State where the said Crimes shall have been committed; but when not committed within any State, the Trial shall be at such Place or Places as the Congress may by Law have directed.

SECTION. 3.

Treason against the United States, shall consist only in levying War against them, or in adhering to their Enemies, giving them Aid and Comfort. No Person shall be convicted of Treason unless on the

Testimony of two Witnesses to the same overt Act, or on Confession in open Court.

The Congress shall have Power to declare the Punishment of Treason, but no Attainder of Treason shall work Corruption of Blood, or Forfeiture except during the Life of the Person attainted.

Article. IV.

SECTION. 1.

Full Faith and Credit shall be given in each State to the public Acts, Records, and judicial Proceedings of every other State. And the Congress may by general Laws prescribe the Manner in which such Acts, Records and Proceedings shall be proved, and the Effect thereof.

SECTION. 2.

The Citizens of each State shall be entitled to all Privileges and Immunities of Citizens in the several States.

A Person charged in any State with Treason, Felony, or other Crime, who shall flee from Justice, and be found in another State, shall on Demand of the executive Authority of the State from which he fled, be delivered up, to be removed to the State having Jurisdiction of the Crime.

No Person held to Service or Labour in one State, under the Laws thereof, escaping into another, shall, in Consequence of any Law or Regulation therein, be discharged from such Service or Labour, but shall be delivered up on Claim of the Party to whom such Service or Labour may be due.

SECTION. 3.

New States may be admitted by the Congress into this Union; but no new State shall be formed or erected within the Jurisdiction of any other State; nor any State be formed by the Junction of two or more States, or Parts of States, without the Consent of the Legislatures of the States concerned as well as of the Congress.

The Congress shall have Power to dispose of and make all needful Rules and Regulations respecting the Territory or other Property belonging to the United States; and nothing in this Constitution shall be so construed as to Prejudice any Claims of the United States, or of any particular State.

SECTION. 4.
The United States shall guarantee to every State in this Union a Republican Form of Government, and shall protect each of them against Invasion; and on Application of the Legislature, or of the Executive (when the Legislature cannot be convened), against domestic Violence.

Article. V.
The Congress, whenever two thirds of both Houses shall deem it necessary, shall propose Amendments to this Constitution, or, on the Application of the Legislatures of two thirds of the several States, shall call a Convention for proposing Amendments, which, in either Case, shall be valid to all Intents and Purposes, as Part of this Constitution, when ratified by the Legislatures of three fourths of the several States, or by Conventions in three fourths thereof, as the one or the other Mode of Ratification may be proposed by the Congress; Provided that no Amendment which may be made prior to the Year one thousand eight hundred and eight shall in any Manner affect the first and fourth Clauses in the Ninth Section of the first Article; and that no State, without its Consent, shall be deprived of its equal Suffrage in the Senate.

Article. VI.
All Debts contracted and Engagements entered into, before the Adoption of this Constitution, shall be as valid against the United States under this Constitution, as under the Confederation.

This Constitution, and the Laws of the United States which

shall be made in Pursuance thereof; and all Treaties made, or which shall be made, under the Authority of the United States, shall be the supreme Law of the Land; and the Judges in every State shall be bound thereby, any Thing in the Constitution or Laws of any State to the Contrary notwithstanding.

The Senators and Representatives before mentioned, and the Members of the several State Legislatures, and all executive and judicial Officers, both of the United States and of the several States, shall be bound by Oath or Affirmation, to support this Constitution; but no religious Test shall ever be required as a Qualification to any Office or public Trust under the United States.

Article. VII.

The Ratification of the Conventions of nine States, shall be sufficient for the Establishment of this Constitution between the States so ratifying the Same.

The Word, "the," being interlined between the seventh and eighth Lines of the first Page, the Word "Thirty" being partly written on an Erazure in the fifteenth Line of the first Page, The Words "is tried" being interlined between the thirty second and thirty third Lines of the first Page and the Word "the" being interlined between the forty third and forty fourth Lines of the second Page.

Attest William Jackson, Secretary

Done in Convention by the Unanimous Consent of the States present the Seventeenth Day of September in the Year of our Lord one thousand seven hundred and Eighty seven and of the Independence of the United States of America the Twelfth In witness whereof We have hereunto subscribed our Names,

SIGNERS OF THE CONSTITUTION

- **George Washington,** President and deputy from Virginia

- **Connecticut**: William Samuel Johnson, Roger Sherman

- **Delaware**: George Read, Gunning Bedford Jr., John Dickinson, Richard Bassett, Jacob Broom

- **Georgia**: William Few, Abraham Baldwin

- **Maryland**: James McHenry, Daniel of St Thomas Jenifer, Daniel Carroll

- **Massachusetts**: Nathaniel Gorham, Rufus King

- **New Hampshire**: John Langdon, Nicholas Gilman

- **New Jersey**: William Livingston, David Brearley. William Paterson, Jonathan Dayton

- **New York**: Alexander Hamilton

- **North Carolina**: William Blount, Richard Dobbs Spaight, Hugh Williamson

- **Pennsylvania**: Benjamin Franklin, Thomas Mifflin, Robert Morris, George Clymer, Thomas FitzSimons, Jared Ingersoll, James Wilson, Gouvernor Morris

- **South Carolina**: John Rutledge, Charles Cotesworth Pinckney, Charles Pinckney, Pierce Butler

- **Virginia**: John Blair, James Madison Jr.